INSIDE AN HONOR KILLING

INSIDE
AN
HONOR
KILLING

A FATHER
AND A DAUGHTER
TELL THEIR
STORY

LENE WOLD

TRANSLATED BY
OLIVIA LASKY

GREYSTONE BOOKS
Vancouver/Berkeley

Greystone Books Ltd.
greystonebooks.com

Cataloguing data available from Library and Archives Canada
ISBN 978-1-77164-437-2 (cloth)
ISBN 978-1-77164-438-9 (epub)
ISBN 978-1-77164-439-6 (epdf)

Editing by Lucy Kenward
Jacket design by Will Brown
Text design by Belle Wuthrich
Jacket photograph by istockphoto.com
Printed and bound in Canada on ancient-forest-friendly paper by Friesens

Greystone Books gratefully acknowledges the Musqueam, Squamish, and Tsleil-
Waututh peoples on whose land our office is located.

Greystone Books thanks the Canada Council for the Arts, the British Columbia Arts
Council, the Province of British Columbia through the Book Publishing Tax Credit,
and the Government of Canada for supporting our publishing activities.

Canada

This translation has been published with the financial support of Norwegian
Literature Abroad (NORLA).

NORLA
NORWEGIAN LITERATURE ABROAD

*In memory of all the women who have been
killed in the name of honor in Jordan.*

CONTENTS

PREFACE TO THE ENGLISH EDITION

T HIS BOOK WAS originally published in Norwegian in March 2017. Since that time, Jordan has taken significant steps toward ending the practice of honor killings. An increase in such killings in 2016 combined with years of campaigning by human rights activists, lawyers, and Queen Rania, and persistent documentation by international and local journalists, may have prompted the authorities to finally take action. Consequently, this book has become both a testament to those who have lost their lives in the name of honor and proof that change is possible. I am humbled and grateful to have been a part of these historic events, but I am also dedicated to continuing my work to put an end to this violence against women and girls.

My aspiration in writing this book was to document honor killings in Jordan, to push forward the removal of article 340 of the Jordanian penal code—which offered to those who commit honor killings the benefit of a "mitigating excuse" that reduces their punishment—and to end the practice of placing women in prison for indefinite periods, a practice known as protective custody.

The past two years have proven that change is possible.

On my last trip to Jordan in December 2016, the Jordanian Iftaa' Department—the General Fatwa Department—issued a fatwa that declared, for the very first time, that honor killings are contrary to sharia law and that such killings are one of society's most heinous crimes.

Consequently, on March 15, 2017, the cabinet adopted reforms recommended by the Royal Committee for Developing the Judiciary and Enhancing the Rule of Law to repeal article 340 of the penal code, and to amend article 98 to prohibit the "fit of fury" defense in relation to crimes committed against females to preserve honor. Honor killings have often been punished more leniently than other murders. Article 340 allows a mitigating excuse that reduces the penalty when a man kills or attacks his wife or any of his female relatives in the alleged act of committing adultery or in "an unlawful bed," and articles 97 and 98 explain how these mitigating excuses can be applied. Article 97 of the penal code states that if the punishment of a crime is execution or life imprisonment and the mitigating circumstances are present, the sentence can be reduced to as little as one year of imprisonment. And article 98 of the penal code provides for the penalty to be reduced when the perpetrator commits the crime in a "fit of fury" resulting from "an unlawful and dangerous act on the part of the victim."

In a landmark ruling less than a week later, on March 21, 2017, Judge Mohammad Tarawneh of the Court of Cassation doubled the sentences for two brothers who poisoned their sister after she fell in love with a man and fled her family home. Their original sentences—seven-and-a-half years' imprisonment for one and ten for the other—were increased to fifteen and twenty years, respectively. The judge stated in an interview: "We want to send a strong message to the people that killing women in the name of family honor will no longer be tolerated by our court." He added that the ruling "will set a precedent and will become the rule in line of which other verdicts in similar circumstances will be handled in the future…This will be the real deterrent to such murders because the exonerating factor will not be regarded by the Cassation Court anymore."

In July 2017, the Jordanian Parliament voted to remove the mitigating excuse offered under article 340 of the Jordanian penal code to murderers who kill in the name of family honor. According to the article, those who would benefit from the mitigating excuse of the article would also not be subject to aggravating circumstances. Later that same month, the chairman of the Legal Committee defended the removal of the mitigating excuse in article 340, saying that the committee supported Jordanian women—and that it was time for Parliament to support them as well.

The first shelter for women whose lives are in danger due to reasons related to "family honor" was opened in Amman in May 2018. Around thirty women were being held at the Jwaideh Women's Correctional and Rehabilitation Centre in "protective custody," which is to say in jail for an indefinite time and without any formal charges. The plan is now to move them gradually to the shelter. According to Raghda Azzeh, who will be the director of the shelter, the ministry has been working for over a year to train the staff in cooperation with local organizations, including Mizan Law Group for Human Rights, which has worked to help release women from protective custody in the past.

***

ALTHOUGH A LOT of positive changes have happened in Jordan over the past two years, only the future will tell if these changes will have real-life consequences for those involved.

Still today, around twenty women are murdered annually in Jordan for reasons related to upholding "family honor."

And still today, courts often reduce the sentence handed down to perpetrators of honor killings because the victims' families request leniency, usually because they are complicit in the killings. Under article 99, the killer's sentence can be cut in half in these cases.

THE LIVES OF girls and women worldwide are still on the line for honor, and more actions are needed to prevent such killings.

The Jordanian state must respect and protect women's right to life, equality, and dignity by following through on penal code reforms, providing victim-centered protection, and combating violence-driving norms and gender discrimination through education and public awareness.

Jordan has the potential to end the practice of honor killings not only nationally but also internationally. Its actions upholding the rights of women and girls could cause an enormous positive spillover effect to other, less human rights–centered countries in the Middle East where honor killings still occur.

It is therefore the responsibility of journalists, activists, concerned citizens, and organizations to monitor the situation in Jordan closely, to hold the government to account, and to continue to push for social, political, and legal change.

INTRODUCTION

I T WAS ONE of those humid, noisy summer nights in Aqaba. The calls to prayer echoed through the turrets of the little Jordanian coastal village located just about two hours south of the ancient city of Petra, at a place on the map where Jordan, Palestine, Israel, and Saudi Arabia all meet. The sounds from outside mingled with the whirring of the ceiling fan that was valiantly trying to fend off the stifling ninety-five-degree-Fahrenheit heat. I lay exhausted on the bed, staring up at the fan's circular movements.

Swoosh. Swoosh. The humid air tickled the beads of sweat on my forehead.

I was thinking about the article I needed to finish writing. I'd traveled to Jordan as a freelancer for the British newspaper *The Independent* after a short stay in Lebanon—which, as a recently graduated journalist, I had decided to leave after forty foreigners were kidnapped and there were rumors of international journalists being captured and beheaded. This was in 2011, during the early days of the conflict in Syria—when these kinds of news stories weren't yet run-of-the-mill, and we journalists weren't yet in the habit of publishing images and videos of our colleagues being murdered. The threat therefore made a strong impression on me, and I was driven to the airport just fifteen minutes before the road was blocked off with burning tires.

The realist in me had been unnerved, but the idealist was still on the quest to document breaches of human rights. I *had* to go back to the Middle East, and promised both the newspaper and myself that I would give a voice to those who weren't being heard. In the world's most well-documented conflict area. Without putting myself in too much danger.

Jordan was therefore the best option. Being there would give me indirect access to the conflicts in Syria, Lebanon, and Iraq, and to the people who were fleeing these areas.

***

THERE WAS A sudden banging on the paper-thin door to my room, and a voice told me to open up. I was surprised; this was my first time in this country. I didn't know anyone here yet and had no idea who the person on the other side of the door could be. Then a man's voice said my name.

"Who is it?" I answered, creeping toward the door and trying to peek through the cracks in the woodwork.

The man banged even harder and tried to turn the handle. I stepped back.

"Open up!" he said, this time more aggressively, and it dawned on me that he was planning to force open the door. There was no way out of the room, no one I could call for help. Screaming or trying to contact reception weren't options. What if he wasn't alone out there? What if the men from reception were in on this? How else would he have learned my name?

I considered climbing out of the fourth-floor window, but it was already too late. The lock gave way and the door flew open. A man entered. As soon as our eyes met, I knew what his intentions were.

I recognized him: he was the large older man who'd been following me all day. He had a gray beard, a prominent nose, a stained shirt, and big, bushy eyebrows. I'd noticed him at the vegetable market outside town. He'd stared at me with a look that went straight through the cloak and hijab I had worn specifically to avoid this kind of attention. He'd shouted after me, smacked his lips, whistled. I'd sped in another direction and ignored him, thinking that maybe the feeling I had that he was following me was just my imagination.

But now he was standing here in my hotel room, undressing me with his eyes once again. I tried to push the door shut but it flung open, striking me in the face so hard I fell backwards. Everything went black. My mouth filled with blood, and I started to realize that this situation wasn't going to end well.

Then, all of a sudden, another man with glasses and a dark beard came in, put his arm around the first man's shoulders, and spoke to him calmly. He led him out of the room and shut the door carefully. They disappeared. Without a glance, without a word.

I lay there, waiting for them to come back, staring at the closed door with the broken lock. I still didn't have anything to protect myself with.

Blood dripped onto the floor as I rose to my feet. Drops trickled down my forehead, mixing with my tears. I took a deep breath, feeling dizzy and off balance. I stood like that for several minutes before cautiously opening the door and peering down the hallway. There was no one there. I was alone, but the fear still wouldn't let go.

***

THIS EXPERIENCE LATER led me to ask questions I had never before considered. What kinds of rights would I have had in Jordan if I had been raped that night? Could I have reported the incident to the police? Gone to the hospital to get help? Processed what had happened and talked about it with family and friends?

I searched for answers. I borrowed books, consulted the Internet, read as much as possible, spoke with imams, journalists, lawyers, and representatives of various human rights and nongovernmental organizations. I even visited prisons. Hospitals. Family homes. Graveyards.

My questions were met with uncomfortable answers. If I'd come from a conservative family and neighborhood in Jordan and been raped that night, the people around me would have said that it was my own fault—and that I could therefore be killed to uphold the family's honor. I wouldn't have been able to report the incident to the police because it would most likely have been interpreted as a breach of family values and Islamic custom. My family could also have accused me of having sex outside of marriage. To take legal action, I would need four witnesses to confirm there had been an assault—which I obviously wouldn't have had. You don't often have four witnesses to a rape.

I wouldn't have been able to tell the hospital what had really happened either, for fear that they would report it to the police. And I wouldn't have been able to tell my family or friends about the incident, for doing so would bring shame to me and my family, and give those closest to me a legitimate reason to kill me. I would, by being raped, have insulted my family's honor, especially if I had gotten pregnant as a result of the assault.

Even the Jordanian legal system would have indirectly legitimized such an honor killing. A husband or close relative who kills a woman in the name of honor gets a reduced sentence—from three months to ten years—according to the Jordanian penal code. If my family had told the courts they didn't want to avenge the killing—which most people in Jordan do choose in these kinds of cases—then the perpetrator would have received a maximum of only a few months in jail.

In other words, if I had been raped and killed in Jordan, the perpetrator wouldn't have been imprisoned for any longer than a few months. In fact, the chance that *I* would have been imprisoned is far greater: some women are involuntarily put in jail or shelters to protect them from being killed by their own family members. One part of the Crime Prevention Law of 1954 gives governors in Jordan the legal right to hold a woman in "administrative custody," without charge or trial, if her release might lead to a criminal act taking place—like one of her family members killing her in the name of honor. Under this kind of custody, a woman risks being held for up to a year, but many end up staying indefinitely because only the governor has the authority to decide whether the threat is reduced enough that she can be released. So, in effect, the punishment is directly transmitted to the victim for the intended criminal act. The women are imprisoned while the perpetrators walk free.

I came to realize that, in practice, this means that— even today—countless women in Jordanian prisons and shelters could be serving time for a crime that never actually occurred. A crime for which *they* were the intended victim. This was a reality that shocked me and that was central to the next four years of my life.

When that stranger broke into my hotel room in Aqaba, I truly felt like something was about to be taken from me. I felt that I hadn't been careful enough, that it was my own fault that I'd ended up in this situation, that I'd been naive for traveling to Jordan as a single woman. I felt ashamed, and like my integrity as an independent woman was threatened. I felt as though it was my responsibility to protect my own body. As though it had been *my* fault that this man nearly managed to attack me.

With that, I got insight into what honor really is, and how it can be taken away. I realized that honor killings are so much more complex than I'd previously believed, and felt that I had a responsibility to investigate the subject further. This time, the story was literally knocking on my door.

***

HOW EXACTLY *do* you justify an honor killing? This question led me deep into Jordanian culture, prisons in Aqaba, and the endless desert of Wadi Rum. I searched through legal documents and news archives for stories about honor killings between 1995 and 2014, and ended up making a list of 139 names. There were 139 women who had been shot and killed, strangled with electrical wires, burned to death, beheaded with an ax, stoned to death, run over, or forced to drink poison—for reasons such as rape, immoral behavior, infidelity, wearing makeup, or simply coming home too late.

The stories were shocking, but I quickly came to understand that I wouldn't find answers to my questions among the victims—for it is only the perpetrator who can explain how you justify an honor killing. Only a father who has killed his own child knows what drove him to do it. Only a brother, a mother, or a sister who played a part in taking the life of one of their own family members knows what thoughts you have in the aftermath. So I decided to go to the neighborhoods where these women had grown up. I wanted to find the siblings, fathers, and mothers who had taken their lives so that I could ask them why.

Over the next few years, I met men who were forced to kill their own mothers when they were only children, boys who were pressured to take their sisters' lives, and husbands who proudly told the tales of how they tortured their own wives to death.

There were many stories, but one in particular stood out from all the others: I met Amina, who survived an honor killing, and her father, Rahman, who had taken her sister's life with several bullets to the head. Their story was unique because I had the opportunity to hear both sides.

I have never been so angry with anyone as I was with Rahman. At the same time, I've never felt so sorry for anyone as I did for Rahman. Because even though he admitted that he tried to kill both of his daughters and succeeded with one, he still doesn't take any responsibility for what he's done. On the contrary, he makes himself out to be a victim of a subculture that places honor over life. This surprised me. If the act were actually carried out for honor, wouldn't he would be proud of what he did?

There is very little honor or pride in Rahman's eyes, however, and his perspective has challenged my own preconceptions. When we talk about honor killings, women are usually presented as victims, men are described as monsters, and Islam itself is defined as the root cause. I now know that this is a rather misleading understanding of a practice that has many other facets. Honor killings have little to do with sharia, the Quran, or Islam; they are about a culture that places honor over life—and culture is something we can challenge and change.

"What leads a father to kill his own children?" I asked Rahman at the end of our turbulent conversations.

"How do you justify an honor killing?" I asked Amina when we met in the desert outside Wadi Rum.

Their answers resulted in this book.

Thank you for everything you shared.

CHAPTER 1

THE RED SHOES

"I WOULD CUT OFF your hands right there," he says, stroking a finger across my wrist before smiling and emphasizing that is exactly what he would do if he found out I was in a relationship with another woman.

I look down at my wrist, my fingers, my ring. Then at the dark brown eyes of the man in front of me.

"Why?" I ask.

He looks at me and pauses before answering. "Because you would bring shame on the family. Because you would deserve to die, or at the very least to lose your hands."

Rahman Abdulkadir takes a puff of shisha and leans back. Outside, the streets of Amman are teeming with activity. Ninety-six percent of passersby would agree with him, according to statistics; they believe that homosexuality is amoral. Ninety-seven percent believe that the state shouldn't even allow homosexuality at all. I myself am unwanted in this country because of my sexual orientation.

"Do you know anyone who's with someone of the same gender?" I ask.

He looks up. "No!"

"How do you know that?" I ask, clutching my coffee cup so tightly my knuckles turn white.

"I'd know it if I met a sinner," he says, adding: "I'd be able to see it their eyes." He shakes his head in disgust.

"Yes. *Inshallah*—God willing," I answer and rest my gaze on one of the minarets in the distance. If I squint, the top of the tower looks like a little hat on the old man's head. A killer wearing a minaret, I think. He looks angry. I squirm uncomfortably in my seat. My shirt is still wet with sweat after running around the Public Security Directorate offices earlier that day. I was trying to get permission to visit the women's prison in Amman, where Rahman's daughter Amina was once held. I think of how absurd an idea that is: that she was imprisoned, while the man who tried to kill her walked free.

***

I HAD SEARCHED for him for over a year. Planned the interview for months. Found all the right contacts. Tried to get in touch with him through various friends and acquaintances. I was about to give up when a text popped up on my phone: he was willing to meet me. I had explained that I was working on a book about honor in Jordan, and that I was interested in speaking with him because he was a respected man with a great deal of life experience—for which he was well known around the neighborhood.

For this interview, I had had to lie for my own safety; I made up a husband and child in Norway, leaving out the fact that I actually had a girlfriend. Many of the women who chose a braver path than me are now lying in Amman's graveyards. They've been buried there to be forgotten, but the nameless gravestones make it impossible to forget that they once existed. The daughter of the man in front of me lies in one of them.

"It's my responsibility to protect my family's honor," he says, his cracked lips slanting upwards as he gestures with his hands.

I shook his hand when I came into the cafe. I politely greeted the person who would kill me if I were a member of his family and cut off my hands if he knew who I really am. Now, his rough hands are fiddling with the mouthpiece of the hookah. His right hand is shaking uncontrollably. It would be an uneven cut, I think, if he were to cut off my hands. He takes another puff of the pipe.

I study his eyes, his wrinkles, his thick beard. I know that he tried to kill both of his daughters over thirty years ago. I wonder what made him torture them as the calls to prayer sounded over Amman's streets in the wee hours of the morning. Had he gotten up earlier and drunk his powerful Arabic coffee? Stared at himself in the mirror one last time before deciding to kill his own children?

I've heard his youngest daughter's version of the story. Now I want to hear his.

"Tell me about your children," I say. "Tell me about your family, your clan, your home."

He looks at me. Opens and closes his mouth. Then he strokes his beard and leans forward.

***

THE FIRST TIME the word *honor* came up in Rahman's life was when he was ten years old. It was a cloudless day in June, and the sun blazed high over the Jordanian desert. Rahman and his older brother, Nasir, stood side by side at one of the marketplaces outside of Ma'an, a small city in southern Jordan well over two hundred miles from the capital of Amman—in an area characterized by conservative Bedouin culture.

Ma'an was an important junction in the 1960s and a natural stopping place for pilgrims from Jordan, Lebanon, and Palestine on their way to Mecca in Saudi Arabia. Travelers from all clans and classes came here—from the Wadi Sirhan in the northeast, Beni Sakhr in the center, Howeitat in the south, and even Palestinian travelers from Beersheba. Only 7 percent of the country's population was still living as migrant Bedouins in the 1960s, but in Ma'an you could see an abundance of the long, narrow black tents that clung to the base of remote mountainsides outside the city.

Rahman and his family didn't belong to a Bedouin clan but lived among a partly settled tribe in the areas around Ma'an. For the most part, they lived in the same place year-round in something that resembled a small village. His parents, uncles, and grandparents on his father's side had sheep and goats and earned their living through barter trade.

It must have been over a hundred degrees that day. Rahman was wearing a light-blue tunic with some yellow spots on it from last night's dinner. Sweat seeped from his skin and sat like little pearls of silver on his arms before they tickled down his body and met the dry desert sand. He was proud to be at the market with Nasir, who was one of the most popular boys at school, known for his deep voice and long, dark beard. Nasir had more hair on his face than the rest of the class had on their heads combined, their father liked to say, adding that he already looked like a fully grown man as a teenager. These comments made Rahman feel small and useless now that he had turned ten and only had four light hairs on his chin.

Rahman loved spending time alone with his brother. Then, he could do whatever he wanted without their father finding out about it. Everything was allowed with Nasir, and as long as they were standing together, no one would ever bother him.

In the little market square, the crowd squeezed eagerly around a hole in the dry sand. The men craned their necks and the women stood on their tiptoes to see better. They clicked their tongues, whispered to one another, moved here and there to find the best place to stand. Nasir took Rahman's arm and pulled him farther into the mass.

Earlier that morning, Rahman had been afraid of going to the market. He'd been concerned he might scream or throw up, or even worse, pee himself. But now, standing here, he wasn't worried about how he would react anymore. Nasir was standing beside him, and he looked like he was more curious than afraid of what was about to happen.

Rahman felt like everything would be okay just as long as he did the same as Nasir.

Down on the street, a coal-black truck bumped along the open landscape. The crowd fell silent and turned en masse. The dust whirled behind the car as it zipped across the plains, leaving a dusty cloud behind it that hung in the clear blue sky.

"Allah be with us," whispered a woman standing nearby, and Rahman saw that her eyes were red.

Rahman thought of Masuma. Of her strange little nose, her eyes that were blue as sapphires in the sun, but green in the dark. She looked different from the other children, and her family had roots in countries other than Jordan. He thought of how she would boast about being stronger than him. "Masuma the Strong" was how she'd introduced herself the first time they met. She wasn't like the other girls. In a lot of ways, she was a bit like a boy. A little boy with a hijab and red sandals.

The truck stopped suddenly at the edge of the marketplace, sending grains of sand over the crowd. The women turned their heads and pulled their shawls over their faces to stop it from getting in their eyes.

Out of the car jumped two men that Rahman had never seen before. One of them had a cloth wrapped around his head and a thick beard all the way down to his chest. The other had a dark scarf that covered his whole face except for a narrow strip for his eyes.

He looks scary, Rahman thought, trying to get a look at the stranger's eyes, which were staring intensely over the crowd.

"The oldest uncle," Nasir whispered, pointing at the man dressed in black. Rahman had been told that he was an educated man, one who could discern right from wrong. Not an ordinary person like Rahman and Nasir's father. He probably came from Saudi Arabia or Iraq, where educated people learned at a real madrasa—a school where one studies Islam.

"*As-salaam alaikum,*" said the man in black, his gaze resting upon a man in the crowd who seemed to be Masuma's father. He was a small, sickly man with deep wrinkles in his dark face. His nose was flat and broad, his eyes red from the sun. On his head was a classic red-checkered scarf called a *hattah*—which most Bedouins wear—with a thick, dark cord on top. He looked sad, but greeted the man respectfully.

The man in black opened the trunk, and two small feet came into view. The murmuring in the crowd began again. The man bent his strong back, lifted the child out of the car, and placed her carefully on the ground. She was wearing a white dress that stood in sharp contrast to the dark-clad man and the brown landscape.

There's Masuma, thought Rahman, noticing that she was wearing the dark red sandals she liked so much, and that were almost brand new.

"Are they going to bury all her things as well?" he asked, but Nasir just looked down at him and told him not to ask such stupid questions.

The man in black told Masuma to walk over to the hole in the sand that was surrounded by the crowd. She looked up at him and squinted into the sun. Then, she staggered forward uncertainly, and Rahman noticed that her hands were tied.

"Why did they bind her hands?"

His brother looked at him and shook his head.

As Masuma shuffled across the desert sand, Rahman could feel the anticipation in the crowd increasing with each step she took. He tried to meet her eyes, but she didn't notice he was there. Maybe she couldn't see him among all these adults. Maybe she was just being aloof. Masuma tended to be that way if she was sad or angry.

He wanted to wave, but she didn't look up. She kept her gaze steady on her shadow and the shadow of the enormous man walking beside her. Maybe she was counting her last steps.

She looks different than usual, thought Rahman. Her hair was unkempt, her body looked worn out.

"Masuma," he whispered, but of course she couldn't hear him over the noise of the crowd.

For a moment, he wished that everything could be as before, that they could meet again—after all this was over. He wanted to hear the sound of her laughter and admire the neat handwriting that adorned her books. Who would he hang out with, and who would cover for him once she was gone? Masuma never tattled on him, never told anyone that he was the one who used to steal the fresh bread her mother had just baked and take it home to his family. Masuma never asked why. She never commented on the filthy clothes he wore, never got angry when he stole paper from her schoolbag. All she did was give him a sympathetic look, and that was that. The only time she got mad was when he teased her in front of the other children. Then *no one* was ever as angry as Masuma.

Maybe they would have gotten married one day, Rahman mused, but now she'd destroyed that chance. She'd committed adultery, as Nasir said, but Rahman didn't quite understand what that really meant. He still didn't know what she'd done to deserve this punishment, only that his father had said that it was terrible to punish a little girl like this, and that people who went to see this kind of thing had misinterpreted Islam.

Rahman peered around him at the men and the women. They all looked like regular people, but none of them had their hair loose or wore dresses like his mother did. The women were wearing *madraga*—a dark outfit that covered their entire body, or *thaub*—a long, dark outfit with different embroideries. The men were clad in traditional full-body tunics in light brown, blue, or gray. Several of the women had shawls covering their heads.

In the middle of the crowd, the man in black told Masuma to stop. She did, and looked up at the throng of people around her. Her eyes were empty; her lip was quivering. She probably thought she was the only child here since she hadn't seen either him or Nasir. He tried to stretch up on his toes again, but she still didn't see him.

"Kneel," said the man in black.

Masuma cast one more glance at the people around her before she squatted down and put her little feet in their red sandals down in the narrow hole. Then, she lowered her body into the hole until her feet met the very bottom. The earth was up to her shoulders now, and her hands lay limply on the sand in front of her.

"Put your arms against your body and look down," said the man. He put his hand on her head and forced her chin downwards. Rahman looked up at Nasir, who was fiddling with the zipper of his jacket and tapping his feet. He kept looking around; surely to make certain that no one they knew had seen they were there. Rahman looked over at Masuma again, and realized that he didn't really want to be here. But now it was too late; he didn't dare leave. He didn't want to be a little wimp. The men around him were chatting and grinning as they pointed at Masuma. They had neither fear nor dread, and Rahman wished he could be more like them.

The man in black pulled out a white shawl that he wrapped around Masuma's head. He covered both her eyes and mouth. When the shawl was in place, you could hear her sobbing. Rahman felt his stomach twinge. What was the last thing she saw? Was it the hole in the ground, or the earth that had been shoveled around her? Or did she remember the eager faces of the crowd that surrounded her? The men who laughed. The women who jeered at her.

Her body was buried up to her shoulders. The man in black stamped the earth tightly around her, the way you do when you plant an olive tree. *Stomp, stomp,* so the trunk stands steady and doesn't tip over. Rahman wondered what it was like being stuck in the ground like this. Whether the ants in the sand tickled her toes, or whether it was cold down there. When he played in the sand, it was often warm on the surface and colder farther down. Masuma's toes must be freezing now.

He felt a lump in his throat and regretted having come here. Regretted that he had defied his father's orders and lied to his mother and said that he was coming home late from school that day because he and Nasir were going to stay and do homework. "Primitive," his father had called the people going to the market to see the execution. "Primitive people who watch others' pain for entertainment."

"*Aib!*—shame!" shouted the man. "Punishment and dishonor awaits those who don't believe. May Allah forgive this child and restore honor to her family."

"What?" whispered Rahman, tugging at the arm of his brother's jacket.

"She brought dishonor upon her family," Nasir answered. "This is about honor—they're going to restore her family's honor."

"But what did she do?" said Rahman, clinging to his brother's arm.

"See that guy over there?" whispered Nasir, pointing at a thin man in light-blue trousers with a deep cut over one eye. He looked like he was around twenty-five. "She tempted him, and they did things, you know, that you're not supposed to do. She insulted her father's honor."

Rahman looked down. He didn't know what kinds of things his brother was talking about, but assumed that it was Masuma's fault that the boy had gotten the cut over his eye. It was her fault that he was standing there now with a sad look on his face. Rahman didn't understand how Masuma could have done something like that to anyone. Had she cut him with a knife, or simply scratched him with her nails? Why had she done that? Was she mad? Or was she a *shaytan*—a devil—who tried to lead men to sin?

"Silence!" shouted the man in black and picked up a stone that he gave to the thin man. The stone had to be about the size of a fist. It couldn't be so small that you couldn't call it a stone, and yet not so big that that it could knock out or kill the person with one throw. Nasir had told Rahman that before they came. The young man reluctantly stretched out his hand and took the stone. He lifted his arm and stared emptily over the brown plains.

"*Shaytaaan!*" he shouted, and threw it at Masuma's head.

Rahman squeezed his eyes together, so tightly that he saw red and black. Now I'm seeing the inside of my own head, he thought as the desert stone flew through the air and made a dull thud as it hit Masuma.

He promised himself he wouldn't open his eyes before it was all over, but his eyelids flew open unwillingly when he heard the first scream. He stared bewildered at Masuma sticking out of the earth. She flailed her head back and forth without any arms to protect herself. A red spot soaked through the white shawl. Then, the man in black raised his arm, and Rahman saw he was holding a pistol.

He closed his eyes again and put his hands over his ears. Forced himself to think of the red sandals that would never be used again. It seemed so wasteful to die with one's shoes on.

***

RAHMAN STOPS SPEAKING and stares apathetically into space. "Islam is a peaceful religion. You Westerners don't understand that."

I stare at him in wonder, thinking that's a strange thing to emphasize now, considering what he has just told me. Of course, I understand that the story thus far has had very little to do with Islam. There isn't a single place in the Quran that says that a faithful Muslim has the right to stone another person. Although stoning is mentioned often, the people who perform this practice are always referred to as infidels. The only thing the Quran says that could come close to resembling an order for stoning is that the Prophet's methods of punishment should be used in cases of infidelity. There is one section in hadith—the stories about Muhammad's life and teachings—that says that the Muslims in the time of the Prophet stoned two people for infidelity.

Stoning is, in other words, only encouraged in various hadiths and sharia—the traditional Islamic jurisprudence based on the mullah's interpretations. There isn't a single chapter in the Holy Book itself that directly encourages anyone to kill their daughters or wives by stoning them.

"What I just told you about Masuma has nothing to do with the Quran or Islam," he says, and explains that honor is a cornerstone of Jordanian society; this is about culture, not religion. Women have *'ird*—propriety, and men have *sharaf*—honor. If a woman loses her propriety, it is gone forever, whereas a man's honor can always be restored. Then, *hamasa*—courage—is important. It demonstrates the family's ability to protect their honor, even if it leads to personal loss and pain.

"So honor killing isn't about Islam, but tradition?" I ask.

"It's about right and wrong," he answers.

My face gets warm. I want to say that I, like many other Westerners, probably understand better than him—a man of sixty-four years who murdered his own daughter—that Islam is a peaceful religion.

"So you think it was right that Masuma was stoned?"

"No," he answers immediately. "She wasn't married. You can't be unfaithful if you aren't married. And you can't stone someone for any reason other than infidelity."

I think about what he is saying. The rules he is referring to are sharia—hence Islam—but the practice of killing for reasons other than infidelity comes from culture and tradition. Even this method of killing—stoning—is quite unusual in Jordan, among both Bedouins and people who live in cities. In fact, stoning is so unusual that this is the first case I've heard of in this country.

"But do you think it was fair to kill her?"

"That is something I can't decide," he answers.

I don't understand why. Masuma's killing and the way it was carried out could never be defended, neither based on the Quran nor on any other religious text. So this culture he is a part of should very well give him enough foundation to know whether he is for or against such an honor killing.

"Masuma was only a child," I say. "How can an innocent child destroy the honor of an entire family?"

"You don't understand our culture," he says, as though "culture" explains all complicated questions.

I sit there anything. He picks at a nick in the table with the nail of his right pointer finger. The same pointer finger that fired seven shots at his own children, I think. The silence between us is tense.

"It's impossible to know if it was right or wrong," he says eventually, and explains that it's hard for him to talk about Masuma's stoning. He was just a child himself when he was witness to the execution, and doesn't know what her uncle or father based their reason for the killing on. Perhaps the sin she was guilty of was so serious that it justified the murder, he speculates.

"How can a Muslim man raised with good Islamic principles justify a murder under *any* circumstance?" I ask.

* * *

"THERE IS ONLY one sin, and that's stealing," Baba said to Rahman and Nasir when they came home from the market. They were exposed before they even set foot in the house. Baba knew something was wrong and asked Rahman straight out what they'd been doing. He couldn't hold back the tears. He thought about Masuma's dead body lying under all the stones out in the desert and of her mother's tearful sobbing.

But now he had a furious Baba before him, tearing at his hair and raging at them. Rahman looked at his father. He was actually called Abd Al-Nasir, after his firstborn son, but they just called him Baba—the Arabic word for *papa*. Both Abd Al-Nasir and Baba were names he usually wore with pride. But not that day. That day, Rahman and Nasir had brought shame over both his names. He was angry—angrier than Rahman had ever seen him before. His bushy eyebrows met in the middle when he wrinkled his forehead.

"Thievery is the only sin! All other sins are a variation of it. There is nothing more contemptible than stealing something that isn't yours, be it a piece of bread or another person's life."

Baba paced restlessly back and forth on the carpet, dust swirling with each step he took. His voice almost quivered as he spoke.

"I'm sorry, Baba," said Rahman meekly and looked over at Nasir, who hadn't shed a tear or said a word since they'd arrived home. "I'm sorry that we lied."

"Entertainment?" Baba looked down at the boys. "Is that how you see it?"

Rahman fretted.

"Was it fun seeing another person die? Is that how you boys have been raised? Are you—my own flesh and blood—primitive people who are drawn in by evil?"

Rahman looked over at Nasir, who was squirming nervously on the mattress beside him. He glanced up at their father and fiddled with a little thread sticking out from his jacket.

"It was Rahman's idea," said Nasir at last.

Rahman froze. Nasir had persuaded *him* to go along. Almost forced him, actually. Had it not been for Nasir, they wouldn't have gone at all. Was Nasir really blaming him now?

"Is that true, Rahman?" Baba shouted, grabbing him by the shoulders and hoisting him up from the worn mattress before he could manage to say anything. "Are you, Rahman, my son, like *them*? Have you forgotten all the principles of Islam? Do you wish harm upon others?"

Rahman felt the words catch in his throat. More than anything, he wanted to cry out "no!"—that it hadn't been his idea to go to the market. That he thought it was awful seeing Masuma die. That he was crying inside and wanted to throw up. That he thought he'd never be able to sleep again. That he didn't understand why she had to die. But he didn't dare speak against his brother. He would much rather face his father's fury than his brother's cold shoulder.

"Allah, have mercy! Do you see what kind of sorrow you bring upon your old Baba?" His father lifted his arm and made a fist. From the corner of his eye, Rahman could see Nasir clenching his jaw shut and turning away.

"Look!" shrieked Baba, kicking at Nasir. "Look! If it's suffering you want as entertainment! See how pain looks in the eyes of someone you love."

Rahman whimpered, looking up at his father and the clenched fist. He stared into his livid eyes and noticed the drops of sweat on his forehead. He saw that Baba meant it. He was really thinking of hurting him. From the corner of his eye, he could see the shocked expression on Nasir's face. Then, the fist suddenly flew toward him and met his nose with a crash, and an indescribable pain spread throughout his body. It was like a fire had been lit beneath his skin. Rahman had of course roughhoused with his schoolmates before, but this was different. Baba had strong arms and was much bigger than him. He had hit him right in the face, without even giving him a chance to protect himself.

"Baba!" shouted Nasir, who had never seen his father use violence before.

Rahman looked fearfully into his father's shining eyes. Then came one blow after another, interrupted only by his father's tearful sobbing as he said repeatedly, "Allah, forgive me. See what I've been forced to do!"

LATER THAT EVENING, Rahman stroked his fingers over a deep cut in his lower lip. It was wet and uneven, but it didn't hurt anymore. Then he looked over at Nasir and held his gaze on a point in the middle of his forehead where his thick eyebrows met.

Lots of hair, but little courage, thought Rahman, laughing inwardly. Now he could stare at Nasir as long as he wanted to. Now he was the one with the upper hand, he who had sacrificed himself for his own brother's cowardice, he who had been beaten black and blue by their own father. Nasir looked sad. Rahman was the strong one now. Younger on the outside, but older on the inside, he thought, and took a bite of the warm bread.

The mood was tense during dinner. What was usually joyful conversation between Baba and Mother was replaced by serious glances and an awkward silence. Rahman looked at his mother's clenched mouth. She was called Sharqiya, a name that reflected the eastern wind that blew the day she was born. She was normally in a good mood, but today she was clearly tormented. He looked at Nasir, who sat staring at his plate, moving a little piece of bread and sauce back and forth mechanically, as though the food might magically disappear if he just moved it enough.

"What's going on with you?" said Baba, leaning toward Nasir. "If I didn't know any better, I'd think you had a bad conscience."

"I feel sorry for Rahman," said Nasir and looked up, as though the lies in his eyes would fall out if he continued to look down.

"I'm fine," said Rahman, meeting his father's red eyes.

Baba looked down at his fists, scrutinizing his red knuckles. He leaned toward their mother, who turned away demonstratively.

"*You* are the one who is the problem, Abd Al-Nasir," she said with disgust in her voice. "If fathers like you didn't beat up their sons and teach their children to use violence, we wouldn't be living in a society where seven-year-old girls are stoned to death because they've been *ightasabat*—raped."

She hit her plate with the palm of her hand and got up. "Don't say that," Baba mumbled. "We're not like *them*."

"You're not any better than *them*," his mother hissed, wrinkling her nose as she said the word *them*, as though it were a sickness. "You are a shame to this family. You defy everything we stand for!" she said, and spat on Baba's fists.

Rahman stared at his mother. He didn't know of any other woman who would treat her husband like this, but then again, his mother wasn't like other women. She didn't wear a niqab or a burka, and she let her long hair hang loose down her back. She always smelled good, like a mix of almonds and jojoba. She often went to Amman to buy beautiful fabrics that she adorned herself with. She even traveled alone sometimes, something very few women would do. "They're envious," she concluded when Rahman said that his friends' mothers gossiped about her.

"Your mother is the bravest person I know," Baba used to say when Rahman lay in his lap, wondering why his mother was so different from everyone else's.

"For the world to move forward, someone has to be different and effect change," Baba explained proudly.

For Rahman, it seemed unfair that it had to be *his* mother who made the world move forward. He wanted to have a mother like all other mothers: one who made as little trouble as possible.

Most people suspected the marriage between Baba and Sharqiya had been a kind of agreement between Baba and his uncle. Baba and Rahman's mother were cousins, and there was an extremely close bond between their fathers.

It used to be common to marry relatives to strengthen family bonds and hold on to the family's resources, but more recently this practice had gone out of favor. Acquaintances said that Baba had married his cousin so that his uncle's dishonorable name could be restored. The uncle had moved from the desert to the city and lived a much more modern life there with his daughters. People claimed that the family's honor was in danger because Sharqiya hadn't gotten married or had children, and was more concerned with studying and meeting friends than finding a husband. They claimed that she would rather live a wild life in the city, and that she wasn't suited for marriage.

His mother and Baba, on the other hand, insisted that they had gotten married because they were in love, and Rahman and Nasir had no reason to think otherwise. The boys' parents still giggled and chatted like teenagers when they crept under the wool blankets at night. Baba made their mother blush with compliments and little gifts from the market, and she got Baba to smile with stories from her life in the city and all the things she'd experienced before they got married. Every Saturday, she would get up extra early to make sweet sage tea that she served Baba in bed. When the steam from the boiling water filled the room and the pale sunbeams danced across the dirt floor, the world was perfect in Baba's eyes.

"You are all a man could want," he would say when she tiptoed across the rug, balancing the hot teacups.

Rahman had been convinced that no one in the whole world was as in love as his parents—until that day at the dinner table when his mother spat on his father's hands.

She rolled her eyes and got up. She wanted some kind of a reaction, an explanation, anything at all from Baba, but he—the strongest of them all, the proud father who always looked after them—just sat there, examining his own fists as though they no longer belonged to him. As though shame was now taking root where his honor once was. A tear ran down his thick beard. His tough father was sitting there, crying.

That was the moment when Rahman knew that nothing would be the same as before. The power dynamic in the family had been turned upside down with a few rough blows delivered on the living room floor. He observed in wonder how he—the smallest of them all—had come out of the situation best. He saw how Baba and Nasir sat there full of guilt, whereas his own conscience was clean. He had learned his lesson, taken his punishment. The pain he felt for Masuma had been beaten out of his body. The wounds he had on his face had already begun to heal. His bad conscience was replaced with restored honor. He was strong, he was brave, and he was no longer afraid of physical pain.

"I feel sorry for Nasir and Baba," Rahman said to his mother, trying to squeeze out a smile that just looked awkward and strange because of the deep cut. She acknowledged his statement with only a brief glance. This was how it was supposed to be, thought Rahman. The bad conscience, everything that was painful and difficult, complicated or intangible, could be replaced with honor. That made honor the most powerful thing in the world, made it worth pro-tecting—at any cost, for any life.

All at once, he understood why Masuma had to accept the consequences of what she had done. It was the only thing that was right, and best for everyone. Both she and her family were better off now.

***

"YOU HAVE TO understand that honor is about collective responsibility and love," says Rahman. A year has gone by since we last met, but Rahman, the coffee, and the conversation are still the same. He explains that all male family members have a responsibility to protect their family's honor, and that no father or mother wants to harm their children, but that you have to set boundaries to teach them the difference between right and wrong.

"But setting boundaries for someone and killing some-one aren't exactly the same thing," I say.

"We are a society that places community above the indi-vidual," answers Rahman. He gestures passionately as he tries to explain the logic behind honor killings. "When someone violates someone else's honor, they have elected to step outside this community. They deprive those closest to them of dignity and value. They have chosen to risk pun-ishment for the activities they involve themselves in." He shakes his head and notes that Western media asserts that Muslim parents *choose* to kill for honor—when in reality it is the children who have the choice between right and wrong.

I reflect on this. He's partly right. The media usually depicts honor killing as a barbaric practice devoid of cultural context and logic. It is often described as a phenomenon that occurs only in traditional societies so far removed from Western moral values that we can't possibly identify with any aspects of them. In reality, however, honor killing is in practice the same as the death penalty; it is a collective punishment in which killing is the reaction to what society has defined as a crime. It is also recognized in part by the state, as Jordanian legislation ensures the punishment for honor killing is minimal, which indirectly gives people the right to take the law into their own hands.

And yet, a person who is sentenced to death in the United States is referred to as a criminal by Western media, whereas someone who is killed for honor in the Middle East is exclusively referred to as a victim. The reasons for this are probably not primarily that honor killings occur outside of the courts or that they are committed by the victim's own family, but rather that the person killed has, in our opinion, done nothing wrong. This opinion, however, is culturally and principally conditional.

Both the attitudes toward the death penalty and honor killings depend on whether or not one believes that killing and violence can be legitimized as a means of punishment or not. And here, we have a great deal of disagreement—among both Jordanians and Americans.

"Are you for the death penalty?" I ask Rahman.

He nods as he explains that he thinks it is justifiable in some cases but that the punishment must be commensurate with the crime. An eye for an eye; that's how it works, he insists.

I try to understand what he's saying. The logic of punishment he adheres to is the principle of retaliation. So if honor and human life are considered equal, then defamation must be considered as serious as a killing. But the purpose of an honor killing is not only revenge but also to restore honor—a kind of compensation.

"So, do you get your honor back by killing another person?"

He considers this. "Honor isn't in the killing itself, but in the family's ability to react," he says, and explains that the grief of losing a child never goes away but that honor is restored when the family stands together against the one who deserves the punishment. It proves that there isn't something wrong with the whole family, for the community's actions say more than an individual's choice.

"Don't you punish criminals where you come from?" he asks.

I look at him and confirm that, yes, we punish criminals in Norway.

"Then you know why we need punishment. What you don't know is how it feels to lose your honor in this country."

***

"ABD AL-NASIR, WHAT a pathetic name," Rahman heard a group of older boys jeer at him on his way home from school. He sped up so the desert sand whirled around his legs as he jogged across the brown landscape.

A long time had passed since the beating—two months, maybe three. Everything had changed. As soon as he started to understand how important honor was, it was torn from him. The boys who were now shouting after him and bullying him used to be his friends. They'd played together, laughed together, shared stories together. But that was before. When Abd Al-Nasir was still an honorable name, and he was still a normal boy.

Rahman thought back to the day his mother had left them and felt the tears welling up. He thought of her packing up her things—her dresses, shoes, bottles of almond oil. Everything was lying in a heap on the floor. He recalled Baba tearfully trying to hold her back, throwing her clothes back in the drawers, clinging to her jewelry so she had to claw it out of his hands.

"Another man would kill you!" he sobbed, as though such a threat would ever work with her.

It was cold that day, Rahman remembered. The sun had sent its first rays down the steep cliffs, but their house was still in the shadows, awaiting the warmth of the morning. He had awoken to utter chaos. Blankets and books were strewn about, and the colorful curtain that split the room into one part for men, one for women, had tumbled down. Their home was being torn apart.

"Greatest of all is love!" Baba had screamed desperately, lying on the mattress and writhing in pain.

"No, Abd Al-Nasir, greatest of all is shame," his mother replied indifferently, without turning to face him. "Greatest of all is shame."

It had been so violent and brutal. In the course of just a few hours, she had packed up the twenty years she and Baba had shared together. She ran back and forth between the white truck and the house, putting all her things in the trunk until there wasn't anything else to get. Until there weren't any of her things left in their home anymore.

Finally, she stood right between the house and the car, in a strange place Rahman saw as being like a symbolic no-man's-land. She shook her head in resignation, as though she were angry at him and Nasir, that they were the reason she was leaving them. That she couldn't bear—couldn't cope with—living with people like them.

"Why are you leaving me?" said Rahman.

"Why don't you want to be my mother anymore?" asked Nasir, tears pouring down his cheeks.

Their mother bit her lip and shut her eyes. Now she was crying too. She said that one day, they would understand. That one day, they would look at themselves in the mirror and see that it was she—and not their father—looking back. She brushed away the mascara running down her cheeks in wide, black stripes. Rahman caught her eye. She shut her eyes again. She turned and left, and didn't look back. As if she didn't even need to say goodbye. As though she'd never even known or loved them.

Nasir had hated their mother's last words. After days of staring into the little mirror that hung in the entrance to the house, he flung it away and promised he would never look in a mirror again.

"I'll just see a whore staring back," he stated, and screamed at Baba that he would never, ever in his entire life become like them. "I hate her and I hate you," he said.

Rahman saw now how hate could grow faster than love ever had.

"Why didn't you stop her?" Rahman asked Baba again and again, but Baba would just look away and start talking about something else to avoid the obvious answer. Other men that Rahman knew tended to say that women had to be protected—not only from strangers, but also from themselves. Baba had failed in his responsibility as a husband and in his responsibility as a father. He had let their mother walk all over them.

And now everything was different. Nasir used to be the most popular boy in school, but now no one even wanted to be seen with him. "Abd Al-Nasir's boys," people said as though "Abd Al-Nasir" were some kind of huge, oozing pustule in the middle of both of their faces. When they walked to or from school, there was always someone shouting at them, always someone laughing and making fun of them.

"Dirty dogs," Nasir used to shout after other children when he was still popular. Back then, they would run like terrified cockroaches across the plains. But there was nothing either Rahman or Nasir could say to help them now. After the first round of bullying, Nasir simply stopped fighting back. He gave up. He stopped defending himself and just let the reality sink in. From now on, they were the lowest on the social ladder. They were honorless, sons of a man who had let a woman control him. Offspring of a man who had let a woman abandon her family. Everything that was painful, everything that tore at their heartstrings—it was all their mother's fault. She had destroyed them.

"Inbreds!" the older boys shouted at them as they formed a little circle with one hand and moved a finger in and out of the hole with the other. One of them made moaning noises, which infuriated Rahman. He tried to close his ears, like his mother had taught him long ago. All the same, however, much of what the boys said hit him right in the heart and stayed there, even long after he'd gotten home.

"Your mother is a whore!" the boys shouted, laughing.

"Bastard!" they shrieked, and the word burned in his mind. "Bastard, bastard!" repeated in his head, back and forth like an unstoppable echo from one side of his brain to the other.

Rahman could feel his blood boiling. It rumbled and hissed. The veins in his throat pumped uncontrollably. He wanted to shout back at the other children, to tell them that his mother wasn't a whore, that she was braver than all their mothers combined, and that soon—in a few years, they just had to wait and see—all other mothers would be like his. More modern. But he knew that was pointless. And what's more—he didn't even believe it himself any longer. No matter what he said or did, it wouldn't make any difference; he was alone against a group of six older boys.

He sped up and looked hopefully toward the next turn. Behind the steep mountainside, the other children wouldn't be able to see him anymore. He took a shortcut through the stony landscape, jogging over razor-sharp this-tle brush that stuck into his toes when he stepped wrong. He looked down at the sandals he'd gotten several months ago. They were already filthy with muck. The stiff soles creaked with each step he took. His mother had given them to him the day before she left. She'd been in Amman and bought the sandals and a light-blue tunic that was a little too big.

"So you have something to grow into," she'd said.

Rahman thought the tunic was incredibly beautiful—nicer than any other tunic he'd had before. He'd given her a big hug and kissed her on the cheek.

She'd brought gifts for both Rahman and Nasir, but this time Baba didn't get anything at all.

Baba. His dear Baba. A "pathetic man," as the other children called him now. No one could understand how a mother could abandon her children this way. In Jordan, it is the women who raise the children, who have responsibility for them, no matter what happens. How could a man raise his children alone? A man's responsibility wasn't the home, after all. Many of his friends' mothers had said she simply *had* to come back. They thought she was just trying to make a point, especially since she hadn't even said goodbye. Rahman, however, thought it was too late, anyway. He didn't want a mother who had left them this way.

Just a bit farther through the mountains, Rahman thought, a few hundred yards, then he would be alone. No other children could shout at him here. No one could get to him with cruel words or threats. Far away, hidden among the enormous sandstone and granite formations, he could vaguely see their house. Safety, as it had represented at one time. The place he had called home from when he first learned how to speak. Now, the building stood like a reminder that his home was made of his parents together, and that one of them was missing. All the smells, sounds, words, and tastes that had once made the house a home were gone. All that was left was a castle of air in the desolate landscape. Empty of family, Rahman thought. Empty of dignity.

When he finally got around the steep precipice, he could see Nasir sitting outside the house, fiddling with a stick in the sand. With big, sweeping movements, he wrote his name, then wiped it away with quick, angry motions. *Nasir*, he wrote, and wiped it away. Rahman stopped and looked at the sad, small figure sitting with head bowed. He wondered if there was something he could do to make him feel better. Nothing had been able to make Nasir smile since their mother had left.

Rahman stopped a bit away from the house. He couldn't see whether Baba had come home yet, but maybe he'd never even left that morning. Maybe he was lying on the blankets and crying. Rolling around in pain and tearing at his long beard, reeking of alcohol, the way he had every day for the last two months.

"Nasir!" shouted Rahman, waving eagerly at his brother.

"Rahman!" Nasir called back, lighting up.

His voice revealed he was happy to see him.

There was belonging, Rahman thought. At least a little belonging between the two of them.

***

RAHMAN SAYS HE has something he wants to show me. We've met several times now. It's September, and the summer sun is making it unbearably hot in the little cafe.

His rough hands fiddle around in his pockets for what he wants to show me. He pulls out a little leather bag, smiling to himself. Then he turns the bag over and shakes out the contents so coins and pebbles clack against the hard surface of the table.

"There," he says, pleased, and picks up a faded photo that he places in front of me. "That's Nasir." He smiles broadly. "My brother," he emphasizes, even though I've already heard his brother's name a dozen times.

I pick up the photo and study it closely. It shows the outline of a stranger who could be twenty or sixty. Impossible to say, as the photo is so blurry.

"When was this taken?"

"The day he got married," he answers quickly. "The day he got married for the second time."

"Two wives," I say. "How many do you have?"

"Only one. I'm more modern that way."

I nod, but don't really understand what he means.

"There is only one woman in my life now," he says, and takes a deep breath.

The deep wrinkles in his forehead pull together in a serious expression. He looks sad. As though the memories from his childhood with Nasir got him to forget how his life ended up, if only for a little while. There is only one woman left in the life of a man who once had three. For a moment, I feel sorry for him.

When you're sitting right across from him, it's easy to forget what he has done, and the way he did it. When he talks about his brother and his family, he seems like a warm and considerate person. I can see the love in his eyes when he talks about his dear Baba, his mother, and his upbringing outside the desert in Ma'an.

"No one could love us like Baba," I remember his daughter telling me the one time we met in the desert. In a strange way, I understand what she means. At times, the man before me *does* seem like a loving father. He has a calmness and mildness about him that you often find in elderly people. His story makes it hard to hate him outright. The way he talks about his life makes me want to understand him, to find an explanation, without that necessarily justifying what he has done.

It looks like he regrets it, but I'm probably the only one who thinks so. In any case, he is a devout Muslim who must fall to his knees five times a day, meet Allah, and ask forgiveness for the life he has taken. I suppose he does do that. He has to. Or doesn't he?

Rahman picks up the coins from the table and puts them back in the leather bag. He folds up the photo of his brother and puts it in his jacket pocket. Then he leans back and meets my eyes.

"What do you really want from me?" he asks. It seems like this seventh meeting has suddenly gotten him wondering why I'm so curious about his life story.

I lean forward.

"I've met your daughter," I say.

His face twitches.

"Do you regret that you tried to kill her?"

CHAPTER 2

THE FIG TREE

IT IS ALREADY dark when my phone rings and a man who introduces himself as Suleiman says he's outside the hotel. I take a last glance in the mirror, making sure my hijab is covering my hair and the makeup is covering up the bruises after the brutal encounter with the hotel door. I'm still shaken after the experience, but have decided that I won't let it stop me.

I put my improvised weapon—a can of hairspray—into my pocket, and activate the location-tracking function on my phone. I send a last text to my sister, like I've done so many times before: "I'm leaving the hotel now. Message the Ministry of Foreign Affairs if I don't text you before nine tomorrow."

I look out of the window at the car and write: "He's driving a white Jeep." Then I add the license-plate number before locking the door.

The adrenaline is pumping through my veins. I don't know if I can trust the men I'm about to meet; I've only spoken with one of them a couple of times before. I told him that I wanted to write a story about honor killings, and he said that he'd be willing to help me. He had contacts in both the prison and the Jordan Public Security Directorate, and would assist as an interpreter and coordinator if I wanted. I said yes. It wasn't long before he'd made a few calls and managed to track down a woman who someone had tried to kill for honor. A woman who had spent most of her life in a women's prison in Amman to avoid being attacked again, and who was now living in hiding. He didn't mention how they knew her or where we were going. The only thing I knew is that she wanted to meet me somewhere in Wadi Rum—the desert near Petra—and that she wouldn't give me her real name.

I walk down the stairs to the reception area, which is illuminated by dazzling fluorescent lights and decorated with a dark brown reception desk and a single computer that looks like it's been there since the nineties. I give my room keys to the men at the front desk and tell them that I'll hopefully be back early tomorrow morning. The receptionist reacts to the fact that I am going out for the whole night, and wonders if the men outside the hotel are waiting for me. I ask if he knows them, and if there is any reason I shouldn't go with them. He shakes his head and says he's never seen them before, but that he thinks one of them works as a tour guide in Petra. I look at the two men outside and ask him to remember what they look like in case I don't come back. He stares at me, his eyes wide.

"But what are you up to?" he asks.

"Work," I say, and continue out the door.

Outside, I see the interpreter and a heavyset older man with a thick, dark moustache and an even thicker waistline. He has a black-and-white checkered scarf wrapped around his head and a dark brown wool coat with a vest over his shoulders. The older man greets me politely as I come out of the hotel.

"I'm Ahmed," he says. He asks if I want to sit in the front or back of the car.

The interpreter greets me as well and bursts into laughter. I look at him, trying to understand what he's laughing at. I've only met him a few times and don't really know him.

"Did you put on your own hijab?" he asks, unable to stop himself from laughing. "You've tied it on wrong."

I laugh as well, partly because of his honest reaction, partly because of my own incompetence, considering I just spent so much time trying to get it to look right.

"It could be the European way of wearing it," says Ahmed and holds his hands in front of his mouth to hold back his own laughter.

"Well, that's exactly what it is, I guess," I say jocularly, brushing away the tears of laughter and opening the back door. The beige leather seats emit a cloud of dust as I sit down. The two men sit in front. The motor starts and a deafening noise fills the old car. Ahmed turns on the radio. Cheerful Arabic music drowns out the racket from the motor and rings out through the empty streets.

We swing out onto the main road and Ahmed says that we have to drive for a while before walking a bit to get into the mountains, where the meeting is taking place. He explains that the woman we're meeting doesn't usually live there, but that I still can't know where we're going. "It's too risky," he says. The interpreter has already explained to me that the woman tends to wear a full niqab to conceal her identity and lives at a secret address because she is afraid that her family may try to kill her again.

"I understand that she has to be careful," I say and peer out the dirty windows. A country that is only a quarter of the size of Norway flies by, a country where Bedouins, Palestinians, and Jordanians have lived for more than eight thousand years, at times fighting against occupational powers, neighboring countries, and each other. Several groundbreaking events in world history and human cultural development took place right here. The area has been occupied by numerous civilizations—some under known leaders like Abraham, Saul, and Pontius Pilate. We also find prehistoric cities from the Stone Age, cities you read about in the Bible that originate from the kingdoms of Ammon, Moab, and Edom. Jesus is said to have been baptized in the Jordan River, and Moses to have wandered over Mount Nebo in Madaba. We find Roman and Crusader fortresses here, and the Nabatean capital of Petra. Today, the ruins in Petra are considered one of the Seven Wonders of the World and display the outstanding agricultural technologies, architecture, art, and written language that were developed here.

Although this country is home to one of the world's oldest cultures, the state of Jordan itself is rather young. It was first recognized as an independent sovereign kingdom in 1946, when the country gained independence from Great Britain, which had controlled the area known at the time as "Transjordan" since the Ottoman Empire collapsed.

Since achieving its independence, Jordan has been the setting of a number of conflicts and wars. The country was directly involved in two wars with Israel in 1948 and 1967, and was strongly influenced by the three Gulf Wars that were fought in the region (in 1980–88, 1991, and 2003). After the war with Israel in 1948, the population of Jordan increased from 400,000 to 1.3 million in one year—mainly due to refugees—which put a great deal of political and economic stress on the country. Another reason for unrest in the country was the Palestine Liberation Organization (PLO), which engaged in guerilla activity in Jordan and Lebanon during the second half of the 1960s. The activity ended in a bloody civil war between the PLO and the government in September of 1970, which was later called Black September. Even though the organization was banned from Jordan after the civil war, the group still managed to carry out several spectacular acts of terror in the country as recently as 1974.

Since then, Jordan has often been on the verge of riots and unrest, a situation that great floods of Palestinian, Lebanese, Iraqi, and Syrian refugees has enhanced. In 2016, Jordan took in over half a million Syrian refugees. In addition, over two million Palestinian refugees are registered in the country, which ultimately constitutes 60 to 70 percent of the population. This creates a highly complex demographic that is further amplified by the fact that Jordan also has internal conflicts between sedentary Jordanians and Bedouins who, over centuries, have lived a nomadic or semi-nomadic life in the desert and steppes.

Despite the demands of balancing such a delicate situation, Jordan is considered relatively stable today. It is an oasis of peace in the Middle East, protected only by the empty desert from the war unfolding on the borders with Iraq and Syria in the north.

"It's hard being a Bedouin in Jordan today," says the driver, turning down the volume on the radio. He explains that he belongs to the Bani Hasan family—the largest Bedouin clan in Jordan—which comprises around a million people.

"So you're a Bedouin?" I ask.

"Yes, just like most of the people who live in Jordan," he answers, looking at me in the rearview mirror. "But the authorities make it difficult for us. King Abdullah isn't fighting for our rights." He explains that the Bedouins have to pay taxes and fees each time they cross the country's borders now, which makes it expensive to live a nomadic lifestyle. Moreover, their goods are worth very little on the open market.

The interpreter turns to face me, interrupting us, and asks if I have a phone or camera. I admit I have a phone and tape recorder with me, and explain that I need both. He wags his finger.

"Give me the phone," he says, reaching his hand toward me.

"Relax," says the driver. "She's writing about *jarimat sharaf*—honor killing—not politics."

"Don't be stupid," says the interpreter. "Honor killing *is* politics. Everything is politics in Jordan."

I look at his outstretched arm and realize that it will be difficult to hold on to my equipment. The interpreter says again that he wants the phone to turn it off, so that the authorities can't follow us.

I look for my phone in my purse and hand it to him. He thanks me, and immediately removes the battery from the back.

"We don't say anything bad about King Abdullah in public," he says, placing the phone and battery in the glove compartment.

"We don't have to talk about King Abdullah," I say.

Ahmed says that isn't a problem. "People are just a bit more careful about what they say publicly now. We have issues here in this country, but overturning the regime like in Egypt and Syria? Never! Without a good alternative, there isn't any reason to take to the streets."

"Do a lot of people speak publicly about women's rights in Jordan?" I ask, trying to redirect the conversation to what we're actually here for.

He thinks for a moment, then eventually says that things have changed a lot in the last thirty years—and that women have gotten some of their respect back.

"I remember my mom wearing a miniskirt and short shorts in the sixties and seventies. All her friends did too." He grins.

I'm surprised. These days, you'd have to look far and wide to see a miniskirt or shorts on the streets in Jordan. Now, almost everyone wears long dresses and a hijab. I would feel extremely insecure if I walked around in a miniskirt, even in the more modern parts of town where hipsters drink organic juice and listen to Arabic rap.

"Were women in Jordan more liberated thirty years ago?" I ask. "Now everyone wears a hijab or a burka. How did that happen?"

"Because Islam has made a strong return," he answers, and emphasizes that a hijab is not necessarily synonymous with oppression.

To a certain extent, I agree with him on that. Most of the women I know who wear a hijab say they've chosen to do so, and aren't being instructed to by others.

"Islam is coming back with such a force because people are disappointed," he says. "Disappointed that both the Western economic system and its politics have failed in Jordan."

It isn't hard to understand what he's referencing. For several decades, Jordan has been one of the West and the US's closest allies in the region, both economically and politically. The situation in the country was quite tense after 1967, when Jordan lost the entire West Bank, which it had annexed in 1948—including rich agricultural areas and important tourist attractions—to Israel during the Six-Day War. The number of Palestinian refugees doubled, and some of the country's most important sources of income disappeared. The situation worsened throughout the 1980s, and social unrest broke out in several cities. When Jordan then affiliated itself with the United Nations sanctions against Iraq after the second Gulf War in 1990–91, it lost aid from the Arab states, and the country was struck by an economic crisis. It became dependent on a considerable amount of foreign assistance, especially from the United States. There was a political parting of ways that many Jordanians interpreted as a step in a more Western direction, and the start of both an economic and moral decline. For many Jordanians, everyday life got harder, with an increase in unemployment and restricted resources.

"So the people of Jordan turned back to religion and tradition when they felt like everything else had failed?"

"Yes," the interpreter confirms. "People lost faith in being able to take control over their own fate, and chose to put it in Allah's hands instead."

This is an interesting consideration. Political parties weren't allowed in Jordan before 1992, and since then the most important party has been the Islamic Action Front, which was closely connected with the Muslim Brotherhood. This movement works primarily for reforms that support a conservative Islamic society and is the largest Islamic organization in the world, despite being outlawed in several countries and labeled as a terrorist organization. Economic dissatisfaction and political instability must have been a breeding ground for more radical voices like this, which could be one of the reasons that Islam has made such a strong comeback, not only in Jordan but across the entire Middle East.

"Does that mean that women's liberation has been put into reverse in Jordan?" I ask.

The two men talk among themselves. Ahmed thinks that women's rights in Jordan are generally good, while the interpreter is in complete disagreement. He brings up the practice of honor killing, explaining that most victims are killed by their brothers or fathers, and that you can't say there are women's rights in a country where women are shot and killed by their own family members.

"What have they done to deserve this punishment?" he asks dejectedly. "Been raped? Walked with a stranger on their way home from school? Or done something else that is so-called 'immoral'?"

"Well, it isn't like it's common to kill someone for that kind of little thing," Ahmed says.

"Yes, it is." The interpreter is getting agitated. "I read an article in the paper about a young woman who was kidnapped and raped. When she was returned to her family, her mother begged the rapist to marry her daughter to maintain the family honor."

He continues to explain that the man accepted the offer and married the woman, but that he divorced her after two years and "delivered" her back. When it turned out she was pregnant, the family had had enough and decided to kill her. Her sister and brother forced her into a car and drove her far into the desert outside Tafileh, where they took turns hacking her with a meat cleaver and hitting her with a rock until she was dead. The autopsy report showed that the woman was seven months pregnant.

"But that isn't something most Jordanians would do," says Ahmed.

"They got seven years in prison for hacking their sister to pieces," says the interpreter. "They would've only gotten a couple of months if they hadn't admitted that they had planned on killing her in advance. *That* says something about the attitudes in this country."

I comment that seven years is actually an uncommonly long sentence when it comes to honor killing, and refer to a case from 2009 when a seventeen-year-old brother stabbed and kicked his thirteen-year-old sister in the head until she died—because she had taken a phone number from an unknown man.

"He got only four months in prison," I say.

"That's what I'm saying," says the interpreter. "The legal system in Jordan oppresses women."

Ahmed shakes his head, but doesn't say anything else.

I sit watching the road twisting and turning through the desolate landscape. It's a cloudless night, and the moon lights up the mountains that surround us. Here, in this open landscape, you can find the origins of Jordan's culture and traditions, I think, and wonder how widespread honor killing actually is, and how often it's carried out in such a brutal way.

We drive for a couple more hours. First on the paved main road along the Dead Sea from Aqaba to Amman, then over a narrower gravel road that gets worse with each mile we cover. Finally, we get to the end. To a place on the map where the road just... stops all of a sudden. A dead end toward the great nothing.

Ahmed stops the car and turns off the lights. We sit in silence for a moment before the interpreter turns to me and says I won't be allowed to see the rest of the way. I look at him in surprise and tell him I really have no idea where we are, and that there is strictly speaking no road to see anymore anyway.

"Get out of the car," he says determinedly, and opens the door.

I look at Ahmed, who winks at me, and I do as I'm told. I open the door and feel the cool night air meet my face. It's starlit and cold. The dry desert air causes both extreme heat and cold, which creates the stark difference in temperature between day and night.

"Put this on," says the interpreter, and passes me his scarf. "Cover your eyes with it."

I look at him, apparently skeptically, as he smiles reassuringly and explains that I'm not allowed to know where we're going, and that this is the only way we can make sure of that. I take the scarf and try to ignore the unease growing inside me.

"I don't know," I say, looking around in distress. "Is this really necessary?"

"We trust you," he answers, and leans toward the car. "And you must trust us."

I look at his brown eyes and curly hair, and glance at Ahmed and my reflection in the window of the car. Then I tie the scarf around my eyes with shaking hands. When I look down, I can only just get a tiny peek of my own feet.

"Come here," says the interpreter, taking hold of the scarf and wrapping it around my head one more time so my feet disappear altogether and I see only darkness. The fabric smells like eucalyptus and tobacco. I feel the warmth of my own breath against it. In and out. Calmly now. The situation is absurd, I think. I'm standing here with two men I barely know, in the middle of the desert in Jordan where no one would ever manage to find me, and now I've even covered up my own eyes.

The interpreter touches my shoulder and I jump, startled.

"Relax," he says. "You can get back in the car."

I feel my way to the door with my hands and sit down. I hear the car door slamming shut and the interpreter sitting down next to me. I fiddle around in my pocket for the hairspray.

The car starts up again and we drive off the bumpy road and across the silky soft sand dunes, and the driver starts singing a traditional song. The sound of his voice breaks what little contact I have left with my surroundings. My body jostles up and down and my head sways from side to side in cadence with the aggressive movements of the car. I have no idea when the big humps will come and sit tensely on standby. I clutch the seat in front of me, try to protect my head. I'm ready for anything. A jump. A touch. A breath. Or the next refrain of what feels like an endless song. All my senses are heightened, and it feels like a strange dream.

"Can I take the scarf off soon?" I ask, and hear the interpreter chortle at my comment.

"Soon," he says, and we drive at least another hour before the car finally stops and Ahmed says we've arrived.

I pull the scarf off my head, get out of the car, and look across the desert. I breathe in the fresh air. The landscape seems endless. Only the dark shadows from the mountains around us mark a distinction between earth and sky. A total lack of demarcation—a stark contrast to the jail cell the woman we're about to meet has spent large parts of her life in.

Ahmed and the interpreter get out of the car, and we walk in silence toward one of the mountains where I can almost make out the shape of a tent. A figure is standing outside, waiting. The mountainsides around us are only stone. Boulders and pebbles of all sizes, sand. Dust on dust. Mile after mile. Nothing lives here. The landscape is dead, I think, trying to collect my thoughts and remember my questions.

When we get closer to the tent, I can see that the figure outside is a hunched older man with years of wrinkles etched into his face. He is wearing a floor-length, dark gray tunic and looks like he's well over seventy. He waves eagerly with his hand, flapping it back and forth to get our attention.

"*As-salaam alaikum*," he says. "Hello. Hey, hey," he says in English. His wide smile reveals that he's missing almost all his teeth.

We greet him, and the interpreter and I are shown into the tent while Ahmed and the old man remain outside to chat and smoke. My eyes immediately meet those of a woman as we enter. They are dark green and framed by a black niqab. She is sitting between large burgundy pillows on a mattress in front of a crackling fire in the middle of the tent. She looks straight at me without averting her gaze, and I notice that one of her eyes lacks focus.

"*As-salaam alaikum*," I say, walking over to her and offering my hand.

She gets up, puts out her own hand, and greets me with a mild voice.

"*Wa alaikum as-salaam*," she says, followed by something in Arabic I don't understand.

"Please sit," says the interpreter and sprawls out on a mattress on the other side of the tent.

"Call me Amina. I've always loved that name," he translates.

"Amina is a nice name," I say.

The scent of sweet tobacco seeps through the thin cloth of the tent. We consider one another in silence. Not even the niqab that covers her face can conceal the abuse she has endured: one of her eyes is clouded over and I can spot a deep scar over her nose. We're both aware that this might be the only time we meet. Neither she nor I belongs in this landscape. Any travel she undertakes can lead to more risk, and she can't attract any attention.

"Is it okay if I record the interview?" I ask, and take my notebook and tape recorder from my bag. She nods, and the interpreter explains to her that I'm the only one who will use the recorded material, and that I will never share it with anyone else. She looks at me understandingly.

"Where do I start?" she asks carefully.

"Start at the beginning," I answer.

* * *

THAT WAS THE summer Amina turned sixteen. It was a beautiful, cloudless day, and the little house on the outskirts of Amman was filled with relatives who had come to eat dinner together. In the kitchen, the women worked over cutting boards, bowls and tubs, chattering away as they chopped up peppers, mint, and tomatoes. From time to time, the scent of spices wafted from the sizzling lamb meat.

Baba and Uncle Nasir were in the garden playing chess in the shade of the old fig tree that Baba was so fond of. Every now and then, they would head to the kitchen on the hunt for the best morsels they could find—a clove of garlic here, a bite of bread there, a tiny piece of the meat resting on huge cutting boards.

"Look at the hyenas," the women giggled, rapping the men across the hands and tossing hazelnuts after them—which sent Baba and Nasir running back to their spot under the fig tree, where they could enjoy their stolen snacks in peace.

Amina stood in the doorway to the garden, taking it all in. She looked at her enormous family in the full swing of the dinner preparations. Everyone had something to do. Her little brother, Akram, was running around setting up all the rickety folding chairs around the even more rickety tables. They had to fix one or two chairs after every party when a plump Auntie Banoush would throw herself into one of the delicate chairs after a round on the dance floor.

Amina watched her brother. He was terrible at both decorating and organizing, which his big sister Aisha was trying to fix by running after him and correcting every single thing he did.

"Stop badgering me!" he whined.

"Then do it *properly*!" Aisha hissed back.

Amina went into the house through the tight hallway, where dozens of shoes testified to how many people were visiting. She walked up the narrow stairway toward the room she shared with her sister, shut the door quietly behind her, and sat down at the chair in front of the mirror. She studied her own reflection, staring at the dark eyebrows and green eyes that were particularly emphasized by her yellow hijab. She loosened the pins on the side and gathered the silk between her fingers, letting the fabric gather in her lap. She removed the hairband at the back of her head and let her hair fall loose. Thick, black hair that billowed over her shoulders.

"Whoever marries you will idolize your hair," her mother used to say when she combed a younger Amina's hair. But now Amina was sixteen. She wasn't a child anymore; soon she would be an adult. The girl staring back at her in the mirror had become a woman.

She picked up the *kohl* from the table and stroked it gently over one eyelid, making a thick black line with steady hands. Maybe some of the young boys from her uncle's clan would come to the party—Nasir's sons and their friends. The strong boys who had grown up in the desert with suntanned faces and powerful upper bodies.

Amina had had a crush on Shahid since she was little. He was the oldest and strongest of them all. He was just like his father, the women used to say. A strong man both morally and physically. Moreover, he was deeply religious and had studied the Quran at one of the country's best schools. Perhaps he would notice her now that she'd gotten older?

She looked at herself. Why had he never noticed her before? The boys in the neighborhood had always shown an interest in her. For them, she was mystical, different, and exciting. Why couldn't Shahid also see that she had become a woman?

"Ah, here you are," her sister said, sticking her head around the door with a wide smile. "You look so pretty."

Amina leaned back in the chair. "Do you think Shahid is coming?"

"Are you still thinking about that Bedouin?" Aisha replied, laughing.

"I'm just wondering if they're coming," said Amina, leaning forward again to finish her makeup.

"Mamma would be overjoyed if you fell for him, you know that, right?"

Aisha disappeared out the door again. "And now hurry up, because they're actually coming soon!" she shouted on her way down the stairs.

Amina pondered how her parents actually would react if she decided to marry someone from her father's clan. Her mother would certainly be overjoyed, but Baba didn't really like the idea of the family following such primitive traditions. He liked to consider himself a modern man.

"A man of the future," he would say. He had chosen to move away from the traditional lifestyle of a desert village for a more modern life in the city. Here he could live without being judged all the time, without being governed by ancient norms and traditions. And yet he had still married her mother, Noora, who was quite conservative and traditional.

Noora came from a well-respected family in Amman. She wore a full burka and niqab, socks up to her knees, closed-toed shoes, and gloves. There wasn't a speck of skin to see—not when she was out, nor when she was at home. She was convinced that the neighbors could see through the windows, and was always complaining how close together people lived here in the city and how little private life they had.

"But in your burka-tent, no one can see you, eh?" Baba would joke. Noora never laughed at that.

The discussions her parents had tended to center on the problems that appeared at the intersection between the modern and the traditional. While Baba wanted openness, Western values, and for his children to make their own decisions, her mother wanted a deeper religious groundwork, more focus on tradition, and a stricter upbringing to give the children a reliable moral foundation.

When Baba wanted the children themselves to choose whether they would wear a hijab or not, their mother had become furious, and the arguing lasted for days. Baba became dejected, yelling and making a terrible racket, while her mother lapsed into passive aggression: first, Baba stopped getting coffee in the morning, then his breakfast disappeared, and eventually he had no plate, glass, or even chair when he went to sit at the table. As usual, the fight ended with Baba making use of the one sentence that won all arguments: "If you want to be so damn traditional, then I demand you submit to your husband's will and put up with my decisions."

"You should be glad that at least there's one person in this house who follows the learnings of the Prophet," her mother snapped back before plodding around the house for hours, trying to decide whether she should follow her own inner voice and keep arguing, or do as she was being told.

The girls for their part spent about two minutes deciding whether or not they would wear a hijab when they finally got the choice. They wanted to be like all the other children at school, and supported their mother's arguments that hijabs weren't about covering yourself up, but rather about opening yourself up for another form of beauty—a beauty not defined by clothes, hair, or makeup. They would much rather be judged on their inner qualities than a superficial exterior.

"Why do you support that oppressive garment?" Baba asked the first times they wrapped themselves in their hijabs. Then, their mother would reprove him by saying that it was strange how this one tradition in Islam—which women had in fact decided on themselves—became the symbol most people criticized and called oppressive.

"Women themselves chose to cover their heads during the time of the Prophet. It wasn't something you men told us to do," she said to him proudly.

"Well, I think it's unnecessary," Baba would reply.

***

AMINA TOOK A last glance in the mirror, fastened her hijab on the side with a pin, and got up.

"Let's go charm some Bedouins," she said to herself, winking at her reflection and giggling. She got butterflies in her stomach just at the thought of seeing Shahid.

Down in the hallway, she heard a hodgepodge of voices and the constant thunk of shoes being kicked off as guests came through the front door.

"Ah, it smells so good," she heard a powerful woman's voice repeat several times. She stole a glance down the stairs, and before she knew it, she was being ambushed by Auntie Banoush and the overpowering scent of her perfume.

"Look at the little one! Look how big she's gotten." Banoush pinched her cheek and laughed so her red lips quivered and her double chin wobbled.

Amina looked over at her older sister, giving her a desperate glance that implored her to come help, but her sister just pretended she didn't understand.

"Nice to see you, Auntie," said Amina, detaching herself from her aunt's grip. Then came stiff handshakes from her uncle and three cousins of seven, nine, and thirteen.

Amina's mother shouted from the kitchen that she should invite the guests in. Amina guided them through the smell of frying meat, mint, and chili out into the garden, where Baba and Uncle Nasir had lit the coals for yet another round of shisha. The young boys eagerly sat down beside them.

"Is Shahid coming?" Amina whispered to her mother, tossing a bit of pepper in her mouth, the sweet juices seeping out.

Her mother looked at her and grinned so that her smile lines came into view around her eyes beneath the niqab.

"Don't give me that look. Just answer me," said Amina, pushing her arm away.

"Why are you so curious?"

"Isn't it polite to wonder who's coming?"

"Ahh, my children have never been so polite before," her mother said before adding, "He's coming, relax."

Amina popped another piece of pepper in her mouth before going out into the garden to chat with the others.

The men were sucking at the hookah and bragging about everything that they'd been up to lately. They always had the same stories: the one about how their father had saved a child from drowning in the river, and how one nephew had saved a whole class from burning in a school. In reality, it was just a curtain that had caught on fire and made a bit of smoke. Everyone knew it, but they still clapped one another on the back enthusiastically and laughed loudly at each other's heroism.

At the end of the garden, Auntie Banoush was wandering restlessly among the tables where the food had been put out.

"Look at Auntie," Aisha whispered, and Amina saw Banoush cram a hand into one of the salad bowls and pluck out a hazelnut with honey that she popped into her mouth. Amina laughed.

"Cheeky little girls!" Banoush laughed when she saw she'd been caught in the act. She fiddled around in a bowl of lettuce leaves and got hold of a cherry tomato, which suddenly came flying toward them.

"Banoush is playing with food!" shouted Amina into the kitchen, catching her mother's eye as she shook her head resignedly.

"Now he's coming!" whispered Aisha, pointing toward the headlights that were casting long rays of light through the glass doors of the entryway. "Now your prince is coming."

Amina poked her sister hard in the side. "Shh! Are you stupid? Don't make this embarrassing for me." She sat down on the stairs, wanting to seem cool and relaxed. She definitely wouldn't be standing in the hallway as though he were someone special to wait for. She would sit here, swinging her new shoes and fiddling with her hijab, and wait to see if he came over to talk to her.

There was a thump from the front door, and she felt a mixture of nerves and bubbling glee that both tickled and made her stomach hurt at the same time. Her mother and all the other women ran over to welcome him. She heard his deep voice and self-assured laughter filling the room. Ever since she was little, she'd felt he was the one for her. She thought of his full lips. She *knew* they were right for one another. No one else had ever made her feel so happy, but at the same time so daft and dumb.

"Come welcome your guests, then, since you're so concerned with being polite!" shouted her mother.

Amina felt herself get annoyed at the comment, but turned around, got up, and walked toward the entryway to do as she'd been told.

Among all the aunts and cousins, the dirty shoes, and the sound of sizzling meat, there he was standing. And *her*! Shahid had brought a girl with him. Amina looked at her. Then at Shahid. Then at her mother, who looked like she was thinking the very same thing. Who was this girl? What was she doing here? Shahid smiled widely, let his dark locks fall across his forehead, and looked at Amina with intense eyes.

"This is my friend Maram," he said, patting the girl on the shoulder.

Amina looked at him carefully, then looked back at the so-called "friend" who was standing in their house with her loose, coal-black hair and fragrant perfume. The girl stretched out her hand and introduced herself confidently. Amina was tempted not to greet her back, but that would be like declaring war, which was the rudest thing she could possibly do. She gripped the girl's hand, leaned forward, and gave her a quick kiss on one cheek, then the other.

"Welcome," she said. "Please make yourself at home."

She regarded Maram, looking at her big brown eyes— quite different from her own. At the wave of black hair that hung loose down her back. She was truly beautiful. If Shahid were with this girl, it wouldn't be strange that he'd never noticed his own cousin. How odd, she thought, to bring a stranger to a family party. And a girl of his own age!

"Come in, both of you," she said, and waved them farther into the house.

Maram thanked her politely and followed the other women into the kitchen, while Shahid disappeared outside among the men, who shortly thereafter laughed loudly at something funny he'd said. That was how it always was; he was always the life of the party.

"How do you and Shahid know each other?" Amina asked Maram hesitantly. She was eager to know whether this stranger was a threat to her potential future or not.

"We met through Yasin, my husband. He's a good friend of Shahid, and coming later this evening."

"So you're just friends?"

"What are you insinuating?" Maram looked at her skeptically.

"Sorry, that was stupid. I was just wondering."

"Do you like him?" Maram asked, giggling.

"No!" Amina protested.

"Yes, she just doesn't know it yet," Aisha broke in, sitting down on the kitchen bench next to them. "She doesn't know it, and he doesn't know it either."

Maram smiled at Aisha and looked at her as if they knew each other already.

"I've seen you at school. I think you're in the year above me," said Maram, putting her hand under Aisha's chin and forcing her eyes up.

"I know who you are," Aisha answered and turned away. "Let's leave it at that."

Amina looked at her sister. What kind of rude answer was that? She peered at Maram, who self-consciously lowered her gaze. An awkward silence filled the room.

"I'm going out to the others," Amina said at last.

THE PARTY CONTINUED with food and music, cakes and candy, and the constant gurgling of hookahs and cackling of women's voices. At one point, Baba had beaten his brother in chess and was celebrating and dancing around the courtyard—but then he lost to Nasir's youngest son and got a candied cashew stuck in his throat. What followed was a tremendous spectacle that ended with Baba lying outstretched on the ground, gasping for air, while Banoush squeezed his chest with her huge hands and finally forced the nut out of his throat.

Aisha and Maram sat chatting in the women's room next to the kitchen while Shahid and most of the cousins sat in the neighboring room. Maram didn't know any of the other women at the party, so Aisha felt like it was her responsibility to chat with her and make her feel welcome. Soon, the room was crammed with women eating, dancing, and chatting. As the evening went on, the men starting playing drums and tambourines as they sang and clapped into the pitch-black night. At the same time, the women danced with their shawls inside the house. Maram and Aisha danced together, dreaming about the men in the garden and giggling at one another's seductive glances and gyrating hips that twisted to the beat of the music. The room smelled of sweet perfumes and mint tea. It had been a fantastic party, Amina thought. Everyone seemed to have enjoyed themselves.

When the guests had finally gone and quiet had once again settled in the little house, Amina asked her sister why she'd been so rude to Maram in the kitchen.

"It was nothing," answered Aisha. "We got along. I really hope she comes to visit us again."

***

AMINA STOPS TALKING and asks if I'm cold. I say I'm fine, but she still gets a blanket and tells me to sit closer to her. I thank her, scoot toward her, and smell the powerful scent of Arabic perfume. I comment that it sounds like she had a nice childhood, and that her family seems wonderful. She doesn't respond.

The old man comes into the tent and puts out dried fruits and nuts, and offers a cup of the piping hot tea that has long been steeping over the fire. The sweet steam tickles my nose when I reach out to take the glass. He says again and again, "Hot! hot! hot!" I nod, and confirm that I won't drink it before it's cooled off. The man grins and disappears out of the tent with the teapot, back to Ahmed and their conversation outside.

"What happened with Shahid?" I ask in Arabic.

"I was so in love," she sighs, clasping her hands to her face and giggling. I notice that the old man reacts to the comment from the opening to the tent. He looks at her with narrowed eyes.

"He doesn't like when I talk about Shahid," she says. "He wants to be the only person I have ever loved."

I suddenly realize that she and this man—surely over thirty years her senior—are together, probably married. I look at her, trying to determine her age from what little I can see of her face, but it's almost impossible. I was sure she was around forty, but now I'm uncertain. Nevertheless, she can't be more than fifty, hence he has to be much older. Maybe he was the only person who would marry her after she was let out of prison: it can't be easy for a woman in Jordan with Amina's history to find a man. Women who have been in prison are stigmatized in Jordanian society, no matter what the reason for their incarceration.

"So what happened between you and Shahid?" I whisper, well aware of how shameful it can be for an Arabic woman to get divorced.

* * *

IT WAS A few months after the party and winter had arrived in Amman. Amina and her sister were sitting at one of the city's highest viewpoints early one morning, dangling their legs over the edge. Amina had been with Shahid almost every day of the two months that had passed, and was completely in love. Of course, the two of them hadn't been alone together, but it was easier to spend time with someone from her own family than it would have been with a total stranger.

She thought about how lucky she was. For many women in Amman, finding a husband was the most important achievement in life. It didn't matter how good your grades were. The ultimate goal was to find a husband with the highest possible social status, who made good money and was well educated.

Nevertheless, even if a man met all these criteria, he could still be perceived as a potential threat to a family's honor. This was because he, with a simple handshake, could destroy what the family valued most: their daughters' and sisters' "purity" and good reputation. Most fathers and brothers considered it their duty to keep this from happening, either by making sure the troublemaker stayed away until the marriage license was signed or by restricting the women's behavior and freedom of movement.

In other words, a relationship with a total stranger could never have developed the way her relationship with Shahid was—unless he had essentially put into writing that he wanted to marry her. But Shahid was their own flesh and blood, someone they could trust. Their honor was his honor. So their parents had allowed them to meet as frequently as they wanted to, as long as someone else went along and they didn't cross any boundaries of acceptable behavior. It didn't matter anyway, though, as they would soon be able to be alone all the time. Amina was almost an *aroos* now, a bride. It was one of the most beautiful words a woman could be called, she thought. The greatest testament to her worth. Shahid had asked if she wanted to marry him. Her success was a reality. Her future was secured. She was young but had already achieved her greatest life goal. And she loved him with all her heart.

"Shahid is going to ask Baba for his blessing," Amina said to Aisha. She expected a great big smile, tears of joy and laughter, but her sister just sat there with an empty gaze, kicking her feet in the gravel.

"Is he?" she asked.

Amina looked at her sister, disappointed by her lack of enthusiasm. Why wasn't she happy for her? This was the biggest thing that had happened to their family since Akram was born!

She looked out over the red mountains and yellow houses that would soon be bathed in the morning sun. They sat there in silence. Before, they could talk about everything, laugh about everything, and share everything, but lately, things had been so strange between them. It was as though Aisha had a secret that could only be dealt with through silence.

"I know you're jealous because you're older than me and still haven't found someone to marry, but I thought at least you would be happy for me."

Amina looked up and met her sister's blank stare and her irritation turned to concern. Aisha was biting her lip, tears streaming down her face.

"Why are you sad?" Amina asked, pulling her sister close to her. Aisha was shaking. She blinked away the tears and wiped her nose with the back of her hand.

"You're right," she said. "I'm jealous. I'm never going to have what you have."

Amina didn't understand what Aisha was talking about. She didn't know how to respond.

"The thought of you and Shahid at your wedding. That you're marrying a man you love. The beautiful clothes and delicious food. Baba and Mamma smiling beside you. The thought just makes me so sad."

"But... I don't understand," said Amina, truly unable to comprehend why her sister felt that she'd never be able to have the same things as her. Both of them were free to fall in love with whomever they wanted and to build the lives they'd always dreamed of. Neither Baba nor Mamma had ever said they needed to have an arranged marriage. Even though her sister was quite a bit pickier than most, she would surely find someone to marry as well.

"Do you love Shahid like you love me?" asked Aisha.

Amina was surprised by the question and explained that it was an entirely different kind of love, that it couldn't be compared.

"But how do you know that it's love?"

"I just know. I know it's something deeper than friendship. What are you so afraid of, Aisha? Just throw yourself into it, then you'll know how it feels!"

"You can't ask me to do that," Aisha replied. "You don't know what this feels like for me." She opened her mouth to say something else, then changed her mind. The moment passed by in the silence, and the wall between them was built up once more.

"I'm weary, Amina. It's not love, what I want. It's not right..."

"What do you mean? What's wrong?"

Amina's throat tightened. She suddenly understood what the problem was. It wasn't strange that the distance between them had grown if her sister was carrying such a secret.

"Are you in love with Shahid?" she asked, looking down. She didn't dare meet Aisha's eyes and see the shame she expected to find in them. A gust of wind snatched at her jacket and she pulled her shawl closer around her. They sat there for a long time, the wind rushing between them. Aisha didn't answer. Did that mean she was right? Who would Shahid choose, then? Could it mean she might lose him? After all, Aisha was prettier—and had better grades.

"It's okay if you're in love with him. Just tell me."

"Let's go back," Aisha answered, drying her cheeks and getting up.

Amina felt the anger building inside her.

"If you really are my sister, then answer me honestly." She took hold of Aisha's shoulder and held her back. "Do you love Shahid?"

"No." Aisha shook her hand off and walked away with quick steps. "No, I don't love your man. Are you stupid?"

"Don't shut me out! Tell me what it is, no one else has to know!" said Amina, following her.

"You can't ask me to do that!" wailed Aisha and sped down the stairs.

Amina walked after her, feeling a thudding in her chest—both out of anger and concern. She kicked at pebbles and tried to get her sister to open up again, but Aisha just pretended she didn't hear what Amina said, pretended she didn't even exist.

They walked home in silence through the steep streets of Amman. Amina didn't know what she should believe, do, or feel.

"Just leave me in peace," Aisha snarled each time Amina tried to talk to her. "I don't want to involve you," she repeated, again and again.

***

WHEN THEY FINALLY got to the courtyard of their house, she saw that Maram was sitting on the stairs and waiting for them. Amina wasn't surprised to see her there; she was always showing up these days—sometimes with her husband, Yasin; sometimes alone. She had been like a part of the family for the last months. She ate dinner with them after Friday prayers and walked with Aisha to school. There was always a good deal of laughter and joy in the house when Maram was visiting. She had an agreeable nature and lit up the otherwise ordinary days with crazy stories about a world that seemed so different. She had traveled to Europe, and often spoke of her experiences there. She was from a much more modern home, and both of her parents were very well educated, yet she still showed Amina's parents respect and understanding. She often had long discussions with Baba, who was overjoyed to finally have someone in the house who agreed with some of his modern values.

Now Maram was sitting there again, smiling at them as they came through the door. Her smile turned quickly to concern when she saw Aisha's red eyes.

"What's wrong?" she asked and embraced Aisha, who buried her face in Maram's dark hair and started to cry again.

Amina shook her head in resignation, patted her sister on the back, and opened the door to the house. She closed it quietly behind her.

She could see the two of them outside through the window. Maybe Maram would be able to talk some reason into her sister. Lately, she felt like Maram had taken her place. Now *she* was the one who got insight into her sister's deepest secrets. *She* who went with Aisha to the tree with the view over the city, and *she* who sat under the fig tree in the garden and stroked her arms. It felt strange that another person had come so suddenly into their lives and so quickly taken the place she had spent her entire childhood building. Aisha had always had trouble opening up. She concealed her own vulnerability by radiating confidence to others, but deep down she was perhaps even more sensitive and sentimental than anyone else Amina knew.

She thought of an episode from when they were children. Aisha was maybe eight and Amina was six. It was a scorching day on the outskirts of Amman, and the humidity almost felt like warm rain against their skin. Aisha was wearing a close-fitting, light-yellow dress that stuck to her body and revealed two enormous sweat stains under her arms.

"You sweat as much with your armpits as your mother cries with her eyes," Baba said playfully, and Amina and her brother had laughed so hard that they almost lost their breath in the cramped car on the road to the Dead Sea.

They played at the beach all day before eating lunch beneath a parasol that Baba had brought with them. They drank cola, which they otherwise were never allowed to have, and ate potato chips and chocolate—something they couldn't tell their mother. These excursions were their little secret. Amina, Aisha, Akram, and Baba.

After the food was eaten, Aisha and Amina lay gazing up at the big parasol. The afternoon sun shone through two big holes at its top. An insect came circling in through one hole and landed atop one of the empty cola cans. Aisha sat up and observed the furry creature. In a matter of seconds, she had caught it in a cup. She begged Baba to let her take it home and show it to Mamma. Baba agreed, as long as she promised to let it go once they got home. The whole way back, Aisha sat with wide eyes and a broad smile. "This will be the happiest pet in the whole world!" she said, giggling the entire way to Amman. When Mamma had seen the insect and it was time to set it free, Aisha couldn't manage to keep her promise. Instead of letting it go, she poured a bit of cola in the bottom of the glass so it would have something to drink. Her disappointment was enormous when she discovered the insect floating upside down in the cola the next day—surely having drowned. "A slow and painful death," their brother concluded. Aisha had stared at him with big eyes, but she refused to show how incredibly sad she truly was. She said nothing to Amina, and then several days later she suddenly threw herself in Baba's lap and bawled and begged Allah to forgive her for taking the life of one of His creatures.

"Allah is merciful," said Baba, stroking her head caringly and rocking her back and forth. "Allah forgives us as long as we ask for forgiveness."

"But can you forgive me, Baba?" Aisha had asked.

"I will always forgive you," Baba answered calmly and kissed her on the forehead. "You should never fear me. I'm your father."

AMINA LOOKED OUT at Maram and Aisha once more. They were still holding one another. She could see Aisha whisper something to Maram. Apparently, Maram had managed to break down the wall Aisha had built up. The same wall that was now keeping Amina out.

***

"YOUR SISTER MUST be very special to you," I say, interrupting Amina's story.

Amina looks down. "I miss her every day. And try to forgive her every day," she replies, and lets the words hang unexplained in the air, to the sound of the water bubbling in the teapot in the background. She looks at the interpreter skeptically. Then she puts her hand on my shoulder and whispers something to me in Arabic that I don't understand.

"What?" asks the interpreter from the other side of the tent where he is lying like a prince atop the soft pillows. Amina says something to him, and he straightens up and says she's asked him to go out with the other men. Amina is going to tell me something only women should hear. He gets up, grabs a handful of nuts, and disappears from the tent. Amina follows after him. She gives the men some matches and a bit of wood and waves them out toward the plains with a graceful gesture. She takes hold of the bit of tent that is fastened to some hooks on the inside and closes the opening. She sits down next to me and takes a deep breath, bows her head, and carefully takes off her niqab.

I first notice the thick, black hair that has been tied back in a tight bun. Then I see the evidence of a story I have not yet been told. Deep scars criss-cross her whole face. One of the thickest cuts goes over her nose and cheek and slices right through the eye that lacks focus. Parts of her chin are gone. Her skin is red and mottled, and her throat black and blue from what was clearly a gunshot wound.

"Who did this to you?" I ask.

"Baba," she says, taking my hand and placing it on her face. "My family."

I stroke my fingers over the scar that goes straight through the soft lines beneath her eyes. I'm shocked that anyone could survive this kind of abuse. Her face is destroyed. She looks at me with her one functioning eye and rests her head against my hand.

"*Inshallah*," she says softly. "God will forgive them."

She lets go of my hand and picks up the tape recorder, indicating that the men outside can't hear what she has to say.

"At home," she says in Arabic and points at the recorder. I nod, and confirm I understand what she means—that the recording won't be translated here by this interpreter she doesn't know but by someone else. Someone who has never met her.

"At home," I confirm, holding my hand over my heart as a sign that it is a promise. She dries her tears and pulls the niqab over her face so she looks just like any other veiled woman once again. The tape recorder disappears beneath the fabric. Then she whispers a stream of Arabic words that I only understand fragments of.

***

THE DISTANCE BETWEEN Amina and Aisha grew with each passing day that winter. By the time summer and fall arrived in Amman once again, Amina had long since given up on the closeness they had once had. Aisha had changed. She had a secret, something she was hiding from her family, and even Amina wasn't allowed to be a part of it—but she saw signs of it each day. Aisha was constantly sneaking out of their room at night. She had to be meeting someone—outside of marriage. The situation was hard for Amina—who on the one hand wanted to be a good sister, but on the other wanted to be a good daughter and tell her mother what was going on.

"Do you feel like Aisha has changed a lot lately?" Amina asked her mother early one morning as they were making baba ghanoush to take with them on a trip.

"Of course she has. I think she's in love, but you're probably the only one who will get to know about that," said her mother, looking at her curiously.

"That's the problem. She doesn't tell me anything anymore. It's like I don't even exist."

Her mother patted her on the shoulder and told her not to worry. Aisha was just growing up, she explained, and said that Amina shouldn't take it personally. Amina shook her head. She felt like everything was about to change, that nothing would be like it was before.

"Give her some time. You'll change as well." Her mother smiled wisely, and quickly flipped the eggplants on the grill.

Amina wanted to tell her mother that Aisha had been sneaking out at night, but decided to let it be. She simply had to stop worrying. Maybe things would already get better that weekend when the whole family was going on a trip together to celebrate that she and Shahid were getting married. Maybe they would have some time to talk together—just her and Aisha—even though Maram was also coming with them, along with her husband and several aunts and uncles.

Amina was looking forward to the excursion. Baba had borrowed a big house from someone who knew Uncle Nasir. The house was close to Aqaba, a small coastal town at the southern end of the country with nice hotels and beaches. On the way down, they would drive through Petra and Wadi Rum and see the sunset over the desert where Baba grew up, but hadn't visited since he moved away.

Baba had always said that this desert was the most beautiful in the whole world. Few people could describe a desert in as many words as he did: the mountains were red as blood oranges, the sand glistened like gold, the rocks glittered like gemstones, and the night sky was filled with sparkling diamonds. For Amina, it just looked like mile after mile of brown sand.

But in this desert, which Baba described as the most beloved in the world, there were also people he spoke of with contempt—a despicable people with dark hearts and deeply wrinkled faces from all the tears they had cried. Baba truly loved the desert, but he hated the people who lived there. He had never explained why. All Amina knew was that he had moved away when he was twenty and never looked back. Not even her mother knew what was hidden in Baba's past, but then again, she wasn't exactly the type who asked questions she didn't want the answers to.

"We don't live in the past and we don't dig up our dead," Baba answered whenever Amina begged him to tell her a bit about his childhood.

"Have some respect for your father now," said Uncle Nasir when she asked him the same questions.

There was surely a reason why they would never talk about their childhood, Amina thought, fetching the jar of tahini and putting it on the kitchen counter. Her mother mixed the tahini with the grilled eggplants, some garlic, lemon juice, and spices. This trip to the desert was probably the closest she would ever come to her ancestors, she thought. These desert-dwelling people her father referred to with disgust as "primitive Bedouins."

"What was Baba like when the two of you met?" Amina asked.

Her mother started to laugh. "He was the skinniest man I'd ever seen. A twenty-year-old man who looked like he was a twelve-year-old boy. A grown man with a bit of fuzz on his chin and a shy gaze. He was the exact opposite of your Uncle Nasir." Her mother chuckled and continued, "They looked like twins, you know the kind where one has taken all the nourishment from the other. Your father looked like he should have been put in an incubator. While Nasir stood there with a straight back, a beard like a lion, and arms like a bear, your father was nothing more than a little gerbil with hardly any hair and protruding eyes."

Amina looked at her mother and started to laugh. She had never heard her talk this way before. "Why did you fall in love with him, then?"

"My heart wanted to take care of someone, and he was basically begging for that. And we weren't the ones who decided it at the beginning, but my father and your grandfather that you've never met. Qadir, who lived with Nasir for a long time out in the desert."

"That's sad. That it was an arranged marriage."

"Not at all. We have a good life."

Amina thought about that.

"Are we going to visit the village Baba comes from?"

Her mother shook her head and looked at her sternly. "No, and don't ask him about that either, Amina. None of us wants to go there. We don't belong there."

Amina grew serious.

"Why not? What really happened to Baba?"

"I don't know. But your father was not easy to live with for the first few years. He was angry. Damaged. It was like something was broken inside him." Her mother mashed the eggplants in a bowl and sprinkled in some pepper. "He was a grown-up man who cried like a baby when he was asleep. Until you kids were born—then he suddenly stopped. I don't know any more than that."

"But he hates his own family, Mamma. He doesn't want to talk about his own father. Don't you wonder about what happened to him?"

"I don't wonder about things I don't want the answer to." Her mother smiled sagely. "And you shouldn't either. You don't have to know everything."

Amina nodded and thought to herself that maybe Shahid could tell her more about her family's history. After all, he was a part of her father's clan. Maybe he knew more than she'd been able to find out. Together, they could figure out what kind of family they were really a part of. What kind of blood they had in their veins.

Her thoughts were interrupted by Aisha bounding down the stairs. She said good morning to them, asked them when they were leaving, and gave their mother a quick kiss on the cheek. Their mother said they were almost ready and that they would leave as soon as they were done with the food. She told Amina to go and find Baba, who she hadn't seen since they'd gotten up.

Amina knew exactly where he was: beneath the big fig tree in the garden. He loved that old tree and sat there as often as he could. She peeked out of the terrace door and confirmed that she was right: Baba sat leaning against the thick trunk with a pipe in hand and his gaze turned up, looking at the foliage. It warmed Amina's heart to see him like this. Even ever-anxious Baba was peaceful and harmonious beneath those leaves. The fig tree was the family's meeting place.

She went out and sat on the bench beside him, staring up at the clusters of figs that hung packed from the thin branches. The fruit was dark blue, almost as black as coal.

"You look thoughtful," she said to him.

He looked at her and told her that he was thinking about the trip ahead of them. "Have I ever told you how beautiful the desert is?"

"Baba, you've told me many times."

"You know the sand isn't like sand anywhere else. It almost glitters. You'll see. It's truly beautiful."

"I know, Baba. I know you think it's beautiful. Is that really what you're sitting here thinking about?"

Baba took a puff of his pipe and made rings of smoke that disintegrated as they met the branches high above. "Did you know that I bought this house with the fig tree to honor my mother?" he said after a moment.

Amina nodded, and asked why this particular tree represented her grandmother so well.

"The fig reminds me that not everything is as it seems at first glance. Beneath the dark surface of a fig, the inside is always red, like blood."

Amina didn't quite understand what he meant but didn't press the matter any further.

"You understand, Amina. Something that is dark—and apparently evil—also has an inside that is vulnerable and soft. Nothing is *only* evil."

"Are we talking about evil figs?" she asked.

"Dark figs and evil people," Baba answered.

Amina considered his words.

"Was grandmother evil?" she asked after a long time.

Baba looked at her with kind eyes. He drew his fingers over his bushy eyebrows and studied her with his wise gaze.

Amina asked him once again if he could tell her something about his upbringing.

"There's nothing to tell," Baba replied. He sat up and explained that there are simple things from the past that you try to forget, that you don't want to pass on to your children. "You want to give the future the chance to live without the pain of the past."

"But you're always saying we have to learn from history, and that people who don't recognize their own mistakes can never move on."

Baba pondered that for a moment. "I guess you're right about that."

He got up and lifted her chin with a finger as he looked down at her with a kind of pained smile. "You're becoming wise, Amina. Remember that those who pose brave questions must also be able to handle painful answers. When you ask something and learn the answer, you can never get your ignorance back."

She looked up at him. The shadow from his body shaded her eyes from the sunbeams that were creeping through the branches above them. She studied his gaze and realized that Baba had a deep secret. There was something he didn't want to tell her.

He kissed her on the forehead and stood up.

She watched Baba's back disappear from the garden and into the house. She got up and followed after him, the questions flurrying in her head.

AN HOUR LATER, the fully packed car whizzed through the morning fog on the way from Amman to Petra, leaving behind it a rumbling echo between the enormous mountains on each side of the valley. Above the horizon, Amina glimpsed a reddish stripe of light toward the southeast. Baba sat in the front, his eyes wide as he looked over the plains.

"Look! Look there, Amina! Look there, Aisha! Look, Akram!" he exclaimed at regular intervals as the landscape changed. "Blood oranges! Diamonds! That's what I was saying! Do you see it now?" He laughed.

Amina looked at the landscape. It was sand. Brown, gray, dry sand. As far as the eye could see. She smiled at Baba in the mirror, looking at the orange light rising on the horizon. "Yes, we see it."

Akram fidgeted in his seat. Baba had told them to take as little with them as possible, but they were still surrounded by bags and baskets and food. Akram was covered in Mamma's boiling-hot wool coat and a silk shawl.

"Ughhh," he groaned. "I never want to get married."

This made Baba guffaw and Aisha started to giggle, and soon the whole car was filled with laughter.

"Weddings are just stupid," Akram continued. "All this commotion. Tons of money. And so many people. And clothes. And food! Nope, I'm never getting married."

Amina leaned forward and peered over at him. "If you keep wearing Mamma's clothes, then you'll never find anyone who wants to marry you anyway," she said, tugging at the shawl atop him.

Aisha giggled as though they were children and smiled at Amina. "Watch out for your competition, Amina. There's a beautiful woman here by the name of Akram who might steal Shahid from you. He's clearly jealous."

"Shahid isn't even a proper man!" their brother snorted. "Not if he wants to marry my gross sister!"

"That's enough," Baba said from the front seat and winked at them. "I can see where this is going."

THEY DROVE ON for another hour and the mood in the car was developing into an apathetic lethargy from the heat. Baba pulled off to the side of the road, parked, hopped out of the driver's seat, and opened the back door.

"Come on, kids!" he said. "Come out and see!"

Aisha, Akram, and Amina poured out of the car, stretched their stiff legs, and followed after Baba toward a little cliff a few hundred yards away. As they walked, Baba told them he used to come to this part of the desert with Uncle Nasir when they were children. This wasn't far from the place they grew up, he explained. His eyes shone with excitement.

"There's a viewpoint over here where you can look out."

They went over to the cliff, which stuck out from the mountainside, lined up side by side like soldiers in a straight line, and looked out over the valley. Amina squinted into the sun that was now high above them in the clear sky.

"Look at it," Baba said, pointing.

In the valley below, there was a row of small tents along a river, which looked like it offered fertile farmland. Small female figures in colorful tunics were squatting and washing clothes there. In the places where the river twisted, it was a vibrant green—in stark contrast to the dry landscape around them.

"It's so pretty," Amina said, taking Baba's hand.

"Doesn't it look peaceful?" he said, looking at her.

"Look over there," said Akram, and pointed at a cave farther down the mountainside. "Can we go look around?" He pulled Aisha with him.

"Be careful," Baba replied, and let them run off. He and Amina stood at the top of the viewpoint.

"Did you grow up here?" Amina asked.

"We had our home here. Over there, where the river turns, was where we had our plot, our animals, and behind the mountain over there to the north was where we went to school. Nasir and I sat here often, just talking. We had a lot of nice times here." Baba smiled.

"It doesn't look like an evil place from here," Amina whispered.

"No," said Baba quietly, his face growing serious. "You can seldom see evil from a distance." He squatted and drew his fingers through his hair. "Amina, I am going to tell you my story, since you're always asking. But don't say that I didn't warn you."

Amina sat down beside him.

"You know that my mother died when we were still small boys?" Baba said. He continued. "Well, she didn't die the way we told you. She mercilessly abandoned us here in the desert with these people. Abandoned me, Nasir, and my father. She just left us."

"Why did she leave?" Amina asked. Baba was finally opening up, and telling her things she hadn't heard before.

"Because of my father. Because he became violent. Because she cared more about her own principles than she did about us."

"What do you mean?"

"She left my father because he beat us."

"So she left you to punish grandfather?"

"She left us, her sons, to punish all of us. And she never looked back. I remember how Nasir shouted after her. She didn't turn around. Not even once. She left like we'd never meant anything to her at all. Like we'd never be able to find her again." Baba shook his head, and his eyes went blank. "But Jordan is a small country, sweetheart. Far too small to hide from your sins."

Amina looked into his eyes. There was something in his gaze she'd never seen before. Something about his voice that was almost mechanical, distant, cold.

"Look here," Baba said, and showed Amina the scar that ran across his cheek. Deep red lines that cleaved through his skin—the scar he had gotten when Uncle Nasir accidentally pushed him into an electric fence. He had told this story as a warning each time one of the children got close to cables or electricity.

"From the fence?" Amina asked.

"No," said Baba, almost soundlessly. "It's from the steel wire I held when we killed her."

Amina started, and sat up straight.

"Be calm," said Baba, quickly moving next to her and putting his hand on her shoulder.

"You killed your own mother?" Amina exclaimed, squirming out of his grip.

"I was just a child." Baba looked at her with stern eyes, and lifted a finger. "You can't tell this to anyone, Amina.

It has to be our secret. It's not like I chose to kill her. I was forced!"

"But you killed her, Baba? Killed Grandmother? I thought she got sick and died!"

"She did." Baba straightened up. "Her sickness was selfishness and shame. No other sickness has taken more lives in this country." He looked at her solemnly, emphasizing again that she couldn't tell this to anyone. "It would destroy me if anyone else knew. It would destroy *us*."

Amina didn't know how to react. She wished that for once she had listened to her mother and not asked Baba about his past. Why couldn't she just let things be? Her beloved father had taken his own mother's life! With his own hands. She couldn't believe it. Would she ever be able to look at him in the same way again?

A tear ran down Baba's cheek. He brushed it away with his hand.

"With my own hands, I forced the wire against Mamma's throat until she writhed so violently that the end of the wire cut my face, and almost hit my eye. I was lucky I wasn't blinded. 'Hold tightly, don't let go,' my father shouted. Mamma gurgled and floundered with her arms. I held on until her body stopped writhing." Baba's voice broke. He held his breath and pressed his lips together. "Afterwards, I lay in her lifeless lap and cried. That was the day my childhood ended. I'm not evil. I did it because I had to. Because I was forced. I was an innocent child."

Amina felt sorry for him. She'd never seen him cry like this before, and was struck by how small and helpless he looked. She put her arms around his neck and pressed her nose into his soft beard. It smelled like safety, just like Baba had always smelled. A mix of freshly brewed coffee and cigarettes. He sobbed heavily, and Amina felt like his whole weight was shoved upon her shoulders.

"I know," she whispered in his ear. "I know that you aren't evil."

Baba took a deep breath and collected himself. He told her that his father and brother had honored him after the killing. That those who had been his enemies became his friends again, and those who had tormented him came to ask for forgiveness. His family became a part of society again after months of being shut out. He shook his head.

"But what kind of society were we even a part of? When I was old enough, I decided to leave this place. I didn't want to be a part of what had made me someone who commits such an act. I didn't want to have children who would experience the same thing. I couldn't forgive myself for what I'd done." He wrinkled his forehead. "The people in this desert are evil. They destroy the good in people before they've even had the chance to grow up. My mother was cruel when she abandoned us, but she didn't deserve to die."

Amina tried to comprehend the pain he'd endured, the burden of such a secret. And how he had managed to bear it all this time. "I won't tell anyone, Baba," she said, and leaned in toward him. "I promise."

Baba held her tightly and rocked back and forth as he'd done when they were children. They sat there in silence for a while, holding each other, before Baba gave her a quick kiss on the head.

"Thank you," he whispered in her ear, and let his gaze wander over the desert once more. Amina looked back at the tiny people down there, living their lives, completely unaware that Baba was watching them from above. The women were washing laundry in the stream, just as generations had surely done before them. They went to their houses, made their coffee, and gathered wood. Maybe these people were even her own relatives. But they were strangers with strange lives and different values, she thought.

"Let's go," she said, and started walking toward the car.

Baba smiled carefully in a kind of half-hearted attempt to mask the pain that was still so clear in his eyes.

***

THE CRACKLING FROM the fire has long since faded and the warmth from the coals is dissipating when the interpreter sticks his head inside the tent. Outside, I can see that the light has changed. The sun is about to rise between the dark mountains in the east, and we should be leaving before dawn. Amina hands me the tape recorder with pale hands.

"You must leave," she says, and sounds disappointed.

"Is it all right if I contact your father?" I ask carefully, failing to meet her eyes. She straightens up and starts gathering the plates and cups—suddenly with rather abrupt movements.

"Why do you want to speak with him?" she says tersely, and I feel that a distance has now grown between us.

"Because both sides of the story have to be told," I answer, and explain that I think his motives are an important part of the story.

She says she's afraid that he'll find her, and that he won't tell the truth. "He's going to deny everything. You have to believe me."

The paraffin lamp on the floor flickers.

I'm not sure how to answer, but I do believe everything she's said.

She turns to me and puts a hand on my shoulder. "I've spent years in prison for a crime that was committed against me, while the men who tried to kill me have lived their lives in freedom. Men always have the opportunity to express themselves in this country. Isn't it time that women are also heard? Isn't my story true before you've had it confirmed by a man?"

I tell her that I agree with her, and that of course I believe her without having her story confirmed by a man. At the same time, however, I stress that I can't accuse someone of murder without giving them the right to defend themselves.

"It also might be the only way we can hold him responsible," I explain.

She doesn't answer.

"How could they keep you in prison for thirteen years for a crime that was committed against you?" I ask.

"If I went free, my family would have killed me. If I'd been killed, the murder would have been my own fault since I had 'provoked' it with my actions. The governors in Jordan have the right to keep women in jail to prevent crimes from happening. That's just how the Jordanian legal system is. It's corrupt and oppressive. The authorities think they're protecting us, but the women lose no matter what."

I'm surprised by what she's telling me. "It's not right that you were in jail while the ones who tried to kill you have been free," I say, and ask again if I can look for her father so he'll be obliged to take responsibility for what he's done.

She considers this question a bit hesitantly, and finishes tidying up around us. Then finally, she calmly says it's okay: I can find him and confront him.

"As long as he doesn't find me. As long as you document what really happened."

She tells me what he looks like, what area they grew up in, and what mosque he used to go to. She waves her hands and speaks quickly, while I try to jot down all the names and details in my notebook. She also asks me to look for the prison she was in so I can see where she spent much of her adult life.

"How can we get in touch again?" I ask, once everything is written down, the tape recorder is turned off, and the interview is over. She looks at her husband in the entrance and evades the question.

"Thank you," is all she says, and she holds her hand over her heart.

I ask again to meet her another time. She just shakes her head, and I understand that this really was the first and last time we'll meet.

We get up, and I stretch out my arms to give her a hug. She leans her veiled face into mine and hugs me carefully around my waist. I feel the contours of her frail body.

"Be careful," she whispers, following me to the entrance and waving farewell.

We walk toward the first rays of sun working their way up behind the meager mountains. I turn and cast a last look at Amina, who is standing in the illuminated opening of the tent. The old man stands beside her. He raises an arm and pulls down a length of fabric that covers the opening.

A closed tent in the desolate landscape.

CHAPTER 3

ONCE AND FOR ALL

AMINA WAS LYING in bed in the little room on the top floor of their vacation home, daydreaming about her future with Shahid. The summer wind played gently with the curtains, and the sound of the waves lulled her to sleep. She fantasized about all the children they would have, their wedding, the breakfasts and dinners they would share. She was happy and sleepy, and lay there listening to the sound of Maram and Aisha, who were still chatting. Aisha suddenly laughed loudly, and Amina looked at the mirror on the wall, where she could see the two girls lying on the mattresses beneath the bunk bed. Her sister was lying side by side with Maram. Their faces were turned to each other.

"Shh!" Maram whispered. "Your sister is asleep. What is it?"

"Nothing. I was just thinking about how things could be if we lived somewhere else, like New York or another city in Europe."

"And that's why you're laughing," Maram said, and pointed out that New York wasn't actually in Europe, but a city in America.

"I'm not just laughing, I'm happy," Aisha answered, putting her nose against Maram's forehead. "I have you; we are here together. What more could you ask for?"

Maram carefully pulled her head away and turned over to her other side. Aisha turned with her, onto her side, close to Maram. She put her hand around her waist.

"Are you crazy?" Maram said, and pushed her hand away. "Your sister is sleeping right above us and your parents are in the room next door. What is going on with you?"

Amina's eyes snapped open, and she stared at the mirror. What did she mean? What were they doing?

"I'm in love with you," Aisha whispered.

Amina could only barely hear her. Her head, heart, and breathing stopped entirely. She didn't dare move. She just lay there with her eyes wide open, holding her breath.

Maram turned around. She looked into Aisha's eyes and stroked her fingers through her hair. Their lips almost touched.

"*Bidde yaki*—I want you!" Aisha said. "They won't hear us. They're sleeping."

Maram shut her eyes.

Aisha continued: "I don't *want* to be in love with you, but I am, and I hate you for it. I feel like I have to choose between you and everything I believe in. Do you understand what I mean?"

They lay there in silence for a while, staring at each other.

"Allah made us different," Maram said, stroking Aisha's back. "I refuse to believe that He is so cruel that he would keep people who love each other away from one another."

"I'm trying to stay away from you, but I can't do it anymore," Aisha replied, snuggling closer to Maram. She leaned forward and kissed her.

Amina couldn't breathe, move, or say anything. She wanted to scream. Suddenly, all the pieces fell into place. She wished that what her sister had said about her was true. That she really had been sleeping and not heard any of this. That she hadn't witnessed her own sister sin while she was in the same room. She squeezed her eyes shut and felt the tears seeping out. How could her own flesh and blood do something like this? Didn't she know what kind of danger she was putting both of them in? How could she choose herself over her family and her faith?

She thought about the Quran, of the history of the prophet Lot. Baba used to read the story to them when they were small. Amina knew it almost by heart: "Do you commit such immorality as no one has preceded you with from among the worlds? Indeed, you approach men with desire, instead of women. Rather, you are a transgressing people."

Amina had been told that the story was about homosexuality. About men who loved men and women who loved women. About "evil" and "ungodly" people who put their own desires above the needs of the community. Even though there wasn't anything written about women who love women in the Quran, it was widely agreed that the story about Lot applied to both genders. Allah sentenced the people of Lot to death for their sins. The Quran was quite clear about this point: There was absolutely no doubt that homosexuality was forbidden.

She shut her eyes and turned away from the sight in the mirror. She tried to disappear inside herself. Unable to do anything, she forced herself to sleep. Closed her eyes, breathed deeply, compelled her mind to another place. The divide between dream and wakefulness gradually became blurry. She fell asleep. Woke up. Fell asleep again. Waited restlessly for the night to be over.

THE NEXT MORNING, she was tormented. She became furious with herself for not stopping them, for just lying there and had not said anything or preventing it from happening. What kind of sister was she if she couldn't even stop her own flesh and blood from sinning? What kind of Muslim was she if she couldn't even protect those most precious to her from the Devil's temptations? She must have done something wrong since Allah was testing her like this. Why hadn't He given her the courage to speak up?

Amina went downstairs to the living room and sat at the breakfast table with the others. She stared darkly at Aisha, who was sitting across from her. She thought of Baba, Mamma, and Akram. Her beloved family. She looked at Maram, and thought how well she had welcomed her and how open her family had been. So naive, unable to really see. This sin had grown in front of their eyes, from their own hospitality.

"Do you want an egg?" asked Baba, passing her the platter of food.

She nodded absentmindedly and took the plate. Why was Allah testing them this way? she asked herself. Allah had created everything, including humankind's innate habits and feelings. People who feel they love someone of the same gender have been subjected to this trial by their creators, and this included Amina as well. But it didn't help to think such thoughts. It was wrong to blame Him, the greatest of them all, for their human errors and omissions. Allah was not evil, He was merciful and generous. How could she blame Him?

Overwhelmed with guilt, she got up from the table abruptly, went to her room, and shut the door.

"What's the matter?" she heard her mother shout after her, but she didn't answer. She couldn't get out even a single word. She kneeled and begged for forgiveness. For the first time in a long time, she turned to Allah. She sobbed loudly as tears filled her eyes. It was so unbelievably painful that someone she loved so much had turned out to be someone she didn't even recognize. How would her family react? Would everything be ruined now? Would her sister be punished? She and her brother become outcasts? Would Shahid still want to marry her? The fear swelled inside her.

Breathe, she thought, rocking nervously back and forth. Maybe it wasn't *so* serious after all, maybe there was something they could do. The questions swirled around in her head. In a desperate attempt to find answers, she took down the Quran from the top of the bookshelf and leafed to the pages where the headings of the various *surahs*— chapters—were listed. No text gave clearer answers than the Quran. Together with the hadiths—the written narratives of Muhammad's life and teachings—it is considered to be the most important source of Islamic jurisprudence—*fiqh*, and these two writings are therefore referred to together as *usul al-fiqh*—"the roots of law."

She read the chapter titles as she had done so many times before when she was a child and her mother wanted her to memorize and recite everything in the Quran. She wasn't allowed to go on to the next *surah* before she had learned the previous one, so she hadn't yet read everything in the Holy Book. The examination of the Quran they got in school was superficial, so she had adhered to the principle of not reading the next page before she had learned the previous one from a scholar who could ensure that her pace and intonation were correct. They often discussed the content afterwards, putting the text into a modern context or looking at how the Prophet Muhammad solved similar situations in the hadiths.

Now she saw the *surahs* in the Quran with new eyes and looked desperately for a chapter that could answer her questions. She used the book as a reference tool instead of the lifework it was supposed to be. She knew it was wrong, but what else could she do? Where else could she seek advice?

She opened the book to the *surahs* she knew and read through the story of Lot in *surah* 11—the one about sodomy and the punishment you could expect for such sins.

She remembered what her teacher had said: Throughout the history of Islam, there were several accounts of people's fates that resulted from their evil deeds. Entire nations were often wiped out by Allah's punishment. The story of Lot was such an account.

Lot was sent to the people of Sodom by Allah because those who lived there were committing a number of sins, including robbery, killing, and sodomy. What made their sins especially serious was the fact that they practiced them openly, without any shame or regret. Lot, however, was a righteous man and commanded the people of Sodom to abandon their sinful way of life to live as Allah had created them. The people refused to change and threatened to banish Lot and his family from the city instead. As the people wouldn't follow His word, Allah decided to wipe out the entire city. He sent two angels to Lot to warn him and his family that the city would be destroyed. The angels came in the form of two beautiful young men who asked to spend the night at Lot's. He reluctantly took the young men in because he was worried that people might attack them. Lot's wife hurried out, however, telling everyone about the beautiful angels they had in their home. Shortly after, a mob of people gathered at Lot's door, demanding he hand over the young men. Lot begged the people not to attack his guests, and even offered his own daughters instead, but they didn't listen. They weren't interested in his women. That same evening, the angels told Lot to leave the city without looking back—and he did as he was told. Then, Allah's punishment came. At dawn, stones rained down upon the inhabitants of Sodom, an earthquake turned the city upside down, and everything and everyone was destroyed.

Amina reflected on this teaching. Islamic scholars had interpreted the fact that Lot's people wanted to disgrace God's messengers (who were men) rather than Lot's daughters as evidence that they were homosexuals. They had further interpreted the fact that stones rained upon them as a directive that homosexuals should be stoned. She read *surah* 26:173, which also mentioned Lot's story and ended with the sentence: "And We rained down upon them a rain (of stones). So evil was the rain of those who were warned." This *surah* explained how the non-believers rejected their chance to be forgiven. Amina had discussed this chapter with her imam when she was younger because she had found it particularly difficult to understand. Although Allah could forgive, there were requirements for those who were to be forgiven. Those who were warned, but who didn't listen to the word of God, were those who chose to be non-believers. They didn't fear Allah and were therefore punished. The way Lot's people responded when he warned them, for example, was like they were asking to be punished. They *wanted* punishment—not forgiveness.

Amina stared at the Quran in her lap. Maybe there was hope? She could warn Aisha. It wasn't too late to change. Most of the *surahs* she knew that talked about homosexuality referenced Lot's story. They described a people who committed many sins, where only one of them was obvious sexual relations between two men. Maybe the most serious crime was a lack of willingness to change your behavior, even if you've been warned?

She thought for a long time. The way she saw it, there wasn't anything in the Quran itself that described love between two people of the same gender. There was nothing other than the story about the people of Sodom wanting to go to men rather than to Lot's daughters, and that Lot feared they would attack his guests. What if this evil wasn't homosexuality? What if it was actually talk of assault and of rape, which so many scholars discussed in connection with this *surah*? Where did it actually mention love between two people of the same gender?

She read through the summary again, leafing through each page, past the *surahs* she had never read before. There wasn't a single place where she could find what she was looking for. She exhaled, discouraged. She had to tell her mother what had happened. She had to ask her for advice. She had to, because she didn't know the answers herself and didn't know what she should do.

"Mamma!" she shouted down the stairs to get her attention.

Her mother appeared in the doorway shortly after. She smiled happily when she saw that Amina was sitting there with the Quran in her lap.

"What's going on? Did you leave breakfast to read the Quran? Was a little bit of egg and tea really all you needed?"

"I don't understand, Mamma. I had a terrible dream last night, about someone I know. And I don't understand it.

Where in the Quran does it say it's forbidden to love someone of the same gender? All the verses about relationships
and marriage are about heterosexual relations."

Her mother looked at her compassionately. "That's
exactly the point. Marriage is between a man and a woman.
All other relations are forbidden. You can't love someone of
the same gender that way. You remember Lot's story?"

"Yes, but there's nothing there about love between two
people of the same gender. I know that Lot is brought up
as evidence that homosexuality is forbidden, but if you
read the story literally, it's more about assault. There isn't
any act of love between two people of the same gender."

Her mother fell silent. She looked at Amina with scrutinizing eyes. "Homosexuality is unnatural. It isn't love; it's
an illness. How can it be an act of love when it extermi-
nates humankind?"

Amina thought of Aisha. Was it really a sickness Maram
had infected Aisha with?

"Do you know someone who practices such sinful
behavior?" her mother asked sternly.

Amina shook her head.

"What if people have interpreted this all wrong,
Mamma? How can love exterminate humankind?"

Her mother snorted. "A society of homosexuals would
exterminate itself. After just one generation, they would
die out. They can't reproduce. There's your evidence right
there. It's a sickness, an epidemic. I don't think there's anything evil or wrong with people who have gotten sick, but
those of us who are healthy have to help them."

Amina nodded. Yes, she could understand that.

Her mother stroked her cheek. "I'll ask you again, Amina. Do you know someone who is sinning? This is serious, do you understand?"

Amina felt her chin and lower lip start to tremble. She knew she had one chance to make a choice. One opportunity to decide who she wanted to be. She could be there for her sister, just as she'd always been there for her before—or let her mother's will settle everything. She could bear this uncomfortable secret alone or share it with her mother and hope for forgiveness. She got up and put her arms around her mother's neck. She hugged her tightly.

"It wasn't a bad dream, Mamma. It was Aisha and Maram. I saw them kissing each other."

She regretted it the second the words left her mouth. The information was like a hand grenade tossed into the air, and a charged silence filled the room as Amina knew that reality would strike with a horrible bang. She felt a terrible uncertainty about who would be struck and how.

"What?" her mother said, her voice shaking. "What are you telling me your rotten sister is doing?"

Amina stared at her in shock. She hadn't expected her mother to react this way. Not so aggressively. Not so strongly.

Her mother grabbed Amina's hands and tried to pull her toward the door to the living room.

"No!" said Amina. "Not now. Not here. Not in front of everyone!"

Her mother raised her finger toward her. Amina saw how her whole hand was quivering with anger.

"Go and get your sister! Get her! Take her down to the beach. Don't you dare do anything else!"

Amina swallowed. She was filled with such deep regret. She had been so foolish to believe that this would be all right, that her mother would understand. Mamma was the most traditional of them all. She nodded obediently. Yes, she understood. She would take Aisha down to the beach.

***

"AL-AQABA PRISON" IS written on the side of the imposing building in front of me. In the days since the meeting in the desert, I have visited several local police stations, looking for women in the same situation as Amina. I wanted to find some kind of documentation, something that would confirm her story. At first, I had had some difficulty believing parts of what she said—especially when it came to the preventive legislation that imprisoned women who were in danger. I thought no law could possibly be designed that way. In the following days, however, I sat with the legal text in my hands, and came to the realization that Amina was right. In Qanon manae Al-jraim 1954, the Crime Prevention Law of 1954, it was written that governors in Jordan have legal authority to keep a woman in "administrative custody" without the case being evaluated in court, if her release would lead to a "criminal act taking place." In a study of the law, it was further explained how this exact clause—which was originally designed to imprison the perpetrator—was being abused to oppress women.

In other words, the punishment for the potential crime is directly transferred to the victim.

I have never before heard of a legal framework that is so discriminatory, and never before heard a story so provocative. I've inquired around Aqaba about whether locals have heard of other women who are imprisoned to avoid being killed for honor. Most people become uncomfortable at the mere mention of the word "honor" but they've told me that such women are first sent to Aqaba Prison, where women and men are held together before the women are transferred to the Jwaideh Women's Prison in Amman. "Proper women" are at home with their families, they stressed.

Perhaps it was a prison like this that Amina was sent to just a few days after her family tried to kill her. It was where she spent her first nights under lock and key. Where the decision that she should be imprisoned for her own safety was made. Where she went in free and left as an outlaw.

I want proof of what she's told me. Although it has been many years since Amina was imprisoned, the police can surely confirm her story. There must be some form of registration, statistic, or official documentation. I stare up at the dilapidated entrance to the prison, which is being overseen by a single guard with a rusty machine gun. Well, perhaps the registration system here might not be the best, I think, but it's still worth a try.

The prison guard asks me to present my UN identification card. I glance quickly at the interpreter next to me, who is clad in a full black suit despite the heat. I've replaced the interpreter who was with me in the desert with this stiffly dressed man, since Amina had seemed so skeptical about the one she'd met. The new interpreter speaks Russian, Arabic, and English and can work as a driver if I need that service as well—which immediately seemed like a lucrative offer, but which I am now regretting. He has told the prison guard that I work for the UN and I have no idea why. By saying that I am someone other than a journalist, he has put me in danger. The authorities could suspect me of lying about my identity to cover up the true purpose of the visit, a belief they could use to put me in prison or deport me from the country if I were to discover some information they don't want to disclose. Jordan has often been criticized for cases related to honor and is likely working hard to keep that information from reaching the international media. The prison I was originally intending only to visit could end up being my new home, thanks to the interpreter's surprising idea.

I search through my bag for a card I know doesn't exist, and feel my pulse rising.

"Here," I say, and hand over an old student ID card from my studies in London. "Goldsmiths" is written in large black writing over a grinning twenty-year-old version of myself.

The guard wrinkles his forehead. He looks at the picture, then at me, and holds the card up against the sun. I look back at the interpreter, who is casually leaning against the prison gate. This was not part of the plan. Ten minutes ago, we had gone over how we would do this step by step, as safely and ethically as possible, but now we are standing here doing the exact opposite, and I have been forced to lie.

"Ali!" the guard shouts, waving the card with the photo of the naive Norwegian girl who believes you can come to Jordan and lie about who you are, just to get into a prison. Inside that worn-out prison wall with barbed wire on all sides is a hard mattress and a cell for people like me. Perhaps they'll imprison me as a spy, or maybe I'll get off with a fine. Perhaps I can talk my way out of the misunderstanding if the interpreter is still on my side. It's difficult to say, based on the guard's expression.

"What's the problem?" I ask as another man comes barging through the front door of the prison and speeds down the gravel path. He is dressed in a dark suit with countless stars on the shoulders. Judging by the number of medals that clatter with each step he takes, he is someone important, someone much higher up in the system.

"Nothing. Welcome, officer," the guard says quickly in English and gives me my card back.

The man running toward us gesticulates and greets us loudly. He apologizes for taking such a long time. "Ali can't read your name with the letters you use. The Latin symbols, you know. It's just gibberish to him." I'm told it's better for me to write my name in Arabic when we're in the office.

"No problem," I say, my heart hammering in my chest.

"Follow me," says the warden, and introduces himself as Omar Mohammed. He turns on his heel and starts up the gravel path. "It's a pleasure to be visited by the UN on such short notice."

I follow the man in black and the *clink, clink* of his medals. I try to breathe, calm down, and appear normal, but the fear just won't let go. I know what kind of place this is, and how difficult it can be to get out once you've ended up inside and don't have the right contacts on the outside.

I have seen the consequences of spending part of your life here. The deep scars, and the empty gazes. The lack of ability to express what has been endured. The indifference for oneself and others in the same situation. There have already been UN investigations into the Jordanian prison system, including reports that document the abuse that has occurred here. If you believe the newer reports, the situation is better these days. The prison warden in front of me probably believes that I'm here to make another report like this.

I look down at the cracked asphalt. Some worker has laid large stones along the edges that mark an artificial divide between what is path and what is desert. A line just as meaningless as the walls that separate those who are free and those who are sitting in prison here, I think. Because these stones and these walls are empty symbols that represent a justice system in which victims are kept locked away instead of criminals.

I walk along the same path that Amina herself may have walked so many years ago. I look up at the same impressive building that almost swallows us in its shadow as we approach it. There is a particular smell here—one that I can't quite manage to put words to. A combination of motor oil and dust. A kind of sour odor that clings to the enormous walls.

I think of how brutal a place like this must have been for a girl of just sixteen. How she was taken up the path to the prison with puffy eyes and quivering lips. How she fell and lay on the hot sand. The sand I walk on now must have stuck to her bloody hands and been the only thing she took with her into captivity. A few rough grains of sand under her nails. A poor memory of a free world outside that was no longer accessible to her. As she neared the prison, it was too late. Too late to turn back. She was trapped.

This image of her has been etched into my memory. Her story has become a part of mine. I am walking in the footsteps of a twenty-five-year-long nightmare.

"So, what are you looking for?" the warden asks, interrupting my train of thought.

"I'm working on a report about women in prison and collecting examples that emphasize the new framework."

He looks at me in surprise, and peers over at the interpreter, who rattles off some phrases in Arabic and grins at the warden, who claps his hands together and laughs loudly. He gives me a wide smile—so wide that almost all of his white teeth are visible. They shine toward me. You should never trust people with such white teeth, I think to myself.

"How have you thought about conducting this survey?" he asks. We walk through the main entrance and I am led through an enormous vestibule leading toward a large staircase in the middle of the building. The white paint is peeling off the worn steel beams. It is strangely quiet inside. As though everyone who is imprisoned here is holding their breath because someone has come to visit.

"I thought I'd interview some of the inmates," I say.

"Interview them here?" He looks at me.

"Yes, here."

"No, *officer*. No, you can't do that." He laughs.

"Why not?" I ask, and pretend that I don't understand how absurd the question is.

"No," he looks at the interpreter and asks if I really mean what I'm saying. The interpreter confirms it all with a short *yes*. The warden's eyes wander in resignation and land on a colleague sitting behind a desk at the other end of the room. "Tea," he says, snapping his fingers. "Get us some tea."

The colleague obeys immediately, pointing at a burgundy leather sofa that is still covered in its plastic wrap, and asks me to sit down. The interpreter and I sit down outside a door with something written in neat Arabic script. The warden looks at me, asks me to wait a moment, opens the door, and slips in.

The interpreter and I are left sitting outside. I look at him and lean back. Shut my eyes and try to sense something. Listen to the sounds, breathe in a smell. It's just like Amina had said. A place where everything is empty. Even the air you fill your lungs with lacks substance. Everything here is dead. And strangely quiet.

"Do you think this will work?" I ask the interpreter, who is busy fiddling with his phone.

"You'll definitely get in," he answers, and pats me on the shoulder. "It'll be harder to get out, though." He grins and winks at me.

I look around me at the pitiful room.

When I met Amina, I asked her what she thought about during those first nights. "About life outside," she answered. "About Baba. About the fact that I was going in voluntarily but that I wasn't allowed to leave."

No one really comes here voluntarily, I thought, and wondered how the police had received her. Today, she would likely be taken care of, but it had been a long time now since she was imprisoned. Surely a lot had changed over the years.

The door opens, and a man with white hair and thick, dark eyebrows pokes his head out and indicates I can enter. I get up from the sofa and go into an enormous office with a table covered with flags and trophies. Behind the table sits the man who greeted me outside the prison and brought me all this way. He speaks to the interpreter in Arabic, who asks me to sit down to the right and explain the purpose of this surprising visit.

It all seems very strange—as though I hadn't just met him outside and explained what I was doing there. I thank him, go over to the chair, and sit down. The man from the other room comes in and puts a cup of tea in front of me.

"I'm working on a report about women in prison in Jordan and was wondering if I could get permission to use this prison as a starting point for a story I'm working on."

The warden looks at me, at his colleague, and at the interpreter, who translates what I've just said. He gives me a wide smile and replies in long Arabic sentences as he fiddles with a gold pen on the table.

"That's a shame," the interpreter translates. "There aren't women in this prison anymore."

I stare at him, thinking that can't be right. At all the local police stations I've visited and asked about women I can interview, I've been told that the women are sent to this prison, where both men and women are placed together before the women are sent on to the women's prison outside Amman. At least three women were sent here in the last week alone to be protected from their families. So if they weren't at the police station, and they weren't in this prison, then what had happened to them?

"So you haven't taken in any women this last week?" I ask the interpreter, who quickly responds that that's what he's been told.

"Where are they then?" I ask.

"We've established a special center for women who want to be protected from their families," he says, smiling proudly. "It's called 'Save the Parents Group.' The women who are sent there say they like it there. They say it's like living in freedom, that they feel at home. If you met them, you'd see it with your own eyes."

I look down, truly wanting to believe what he's saying is true, but it simply can't be. Not only is the name he probably just made up absurd, but I already know that no such place exists.

"Where can I meet them?" I ask.

"Well, they live at a secret address, of course. That's the whole point. That it's secret." He squirms restlessly in his chair. "This prison takes very good care of women—

I mean, if one came here for some reason or another, but they don't."

"But women have come here before?" I ask the interpreter.

The warden avoids the question again. "We put women in prison to prevent crimes from taking place. Yes, we imprison them. It's preventive. If you ask me why we imprison women when they're the ones being threatened, well, that's obvious. They are the ones provoking criminal behavior."

So this is the explanation behind the Crime Prevention Law of 1954, I think. They imprison the women to prevent them from being killed. Not the potential perpetrator who wants to kill them. Preventive, possibly, but not in the least bit fair. I ask once again if that means that there are women in this prison who are being protected from such a criminal act.

He sighs in resignation, picks up his phone, and dials a number. He puts the phone on speaker and lets the dial tone fill the room.

"See," he says. "No women at home."

I laugh, but his dark eyes tell me that this isn't a joke. He sincerely believes this is proof that there aren't any women here.

"Can I see what the cells in the prison look like?" I ask.

"No," he says, and sits up. "We protect the identities of the people in here."

"What about the cells the women were in? They must be empty now that no one is there."

"There are men in them now. I can promise you don't want to go in there. It would be dangerous for you."

I look at him and lean forward. "According to the local police, three women were sent here in the last week. What happened to them?"

The interpreter looks at me, shakes his head, and refuses to translate. He explains that the question sounds like an accusation. It's rude. "Way too direct," he whispers.

Then the warden suddenly responds in flawless English: "I think we're done now, Miss. Thank you for the visit."

I stare at him in astonishment. The man can speak English. Why have we been sitting here with an interpreter and complicating the situation, then?

"It's best you go now," he says, getting up and extending his hand.

"We appreciate your cooperation," he says, and insists that we take a picture in front of the photo of the king that he has hanging on the wall, as proof that this meeting really did take place.

I get up reluctantly, and in a last attempt to get some information ask if he can confirm that Amina has been imprisoned here.

"No. I've never said or heard that name before. We don't have women here, like I said."

"What about a register, surveys, statistics? Is there anything at all I can get access to?"

He goes over to the bench by the table and takes out an information pamphlet about the prison from 2001 that I've already downloaded online.

"Here," he says, and shakes my hand contentedly. "Here's everything I can give you."

I shake my head in resignation, arrange myself between the three men, and am photographed with a smile that is just as fake as his white teeth.

"It's very quiet in your prison," I say afterwards. I thank him for the visit, turn abruptly, and leave.

***

"WHAT HAVE YOU done, you shameless dog?" her mother shouted. Aisha's breath wheezed in her chest and her eyes were as wide as the eyes of the cows that were sometimes slaughtered in the town square. It was a look without hope, Amina thought. A look that seemed to be reconciled with whatever might happen, but at the same time feared the pain that would come along with it.

Amina tried not to meet Aisha's eyes. She didn't want to be confronted with the shame of having tattled on her own sister. She wished she could just disappear. Vanish from the narrow beach surrounded by stones and thorns. Escape from Aisha and her mother. She wanted to run across the dry hillside up to the house, past the breakfast table where Aisha's tea was going cold. She wanted to run to her bed, get under the covers, and hide there until this was all over. But each time she tried to move, her mother glared at her and made sure she stayed.

Her mother shoved Aisha, screaming at her. A push here, a blow there. Aisha stood still with her head bowed, without trying to protect herself. Her mother grabbed her daughter's wrists and held them so hard her knuckles turned white. She screamed in Aisha's face and shook her. Amina didn't even hear what was being said; it felt like she was having an out-of-body experience. The words were like a steady stream of indistinguishable sound. Her mother's eyes were almost black, and Amina saw something there she'd never seen before. She thought it was hatred.

Aisha kneeled before their mother, begging for forgiveness, but her mother just pushed her away. She fell backwards and landed on her back. She coughed, lying with her arms in front of her face to protect herself. Her mother, standing above with balled fists, just looked at her. Then she bent down and forced Aisha's eyes open with the tips of her fingers, almost digging them out, and stared her in the eyes.

"If you meet her one more time, I swear on the Prophet's name that we will find you. And when we do, there won't be a court in this godforsaken country that will hold us responsible for what we will do to you. Do you understand?" She got up and spat on Aisha three times. "You are no longer my daughter."

Amina wanted to sit down on the ground next to Aisha and put her arms over her head, but she didn't dare.

"That's enough now, Mamma," she said instead with a weak voice.

Her mother just looked at her. She stood there in her coal-black burka with two ice-cold eyes peering out, looking like the Angel of Death.

"Enough now?" her mother snarled. "You think it's enough now? I haven't even said anything to your father yet."

Aisha opened her eyes and the tears poured out. She sobbed. Amina went over to her and sat down. She pulled her close and rocked her back and forth as she stroked her hand over her head. She said that Allah would forgive her, that Allah knew mercy, that this was just a test.

"She can't help it, Mamma. She was born this way. She needs help. You said it yourself."

"Homosexuality is not something you are born with, Amina! You aren't born sick. We are all born healthy. If you get sick, you can't just get rid of the symptoms—you have to get rid of the whole sickness."

"What kind of thing is that to say?" Amina protested. "Some children *are* born sick."

"No. Sick children should not be born. They aren't suitable for this life! They're just a burden on the family, don't you see that?"

Aisha burst into tears and shouted at their mother: "So you wish I'd never been born? You want to kill me?"

Her mother snorted.

"Honor killings are deliberate and planned, Aisha. They're not like crimes of passion or jealousy."

Aisha sat up straight in anger and dried away her tears. "I thought you were my mother! That you would protect me! Islam has goodwill and room for mistakes. Who are you to judge me?"

Her mother nodded. "You're right. There are plenty of pills at the pharmacy and knives in the kitchen for you to take responsibility for your own sins. Do you hear me?" She leaned down again and grabbed at Aisha's hijab. She tore it off her head with violent movements. "You may not fear Allah, but no one can be sure of what He will do! You may have made your choice, but our family is stronger than you."

She began to recite the Quran like a judge unwaveringly passing a sentence.

"God's mercy is only for those who make mistakes in ignorance and immediately regret them," she said, looking down at both of them in triumph. As though what she had just said was in her own interest. As if this were a fact from the quiz book she read from on Saturdays beneath the fig tree—with a final answer that proved that she was right and they were wrong.

"According to sharia, homosexuality and pedophilia are obscene, dirty, and shameless, Aisha! How could you?"

She gathered the fabric from the hijab in her hands, threw it at Aisha, turned her back to them, and walked away.

Aisha was still lying in Amina's lap.

"You tattled on me," Aisha said, shaking her head. "You betrayed me."

Aisha felt her stomach knot up.

"But they won't kill me. Baba won't do that. He's not like them."

She said it with such strong conviction that it made Amina's heart hurt.

***

"*ALLAHU AKBAR*—GOD IS great," crackles from the speakers atop the narrow towers that surround me in the mosque.

"Ashhadu anna Muhammadan-rasulullah—And Muhammad is His messenger," rings over downtown Amman from one minaret to the next. I've gotten used to the calls to prayer. It's the third time I'm in Jordan, and what used to feel strange and foreign has become a part of my daily routine. I wake to the first prayers at dawn, go to the gym with my burka-clad friends, drink Arabic coffee and smoke shisha at my favorite cafe, and know where I can find the city's best falafel. According to my closest friends, the fact that I have found my own favorite falafel place is the real proof that I've become a true Arab.

I peer up at the enormous building covered in blue terra-cotta tiles. It's actually named the King Abdullah Mosque because it was built in honor of King Abdullah I, but most people just call it the Blue Mosque, and it's easy to understand why. The building is a beautiful sight in this otherwise colorless part of town.

The first time I was here, I was surprised to find two churches next to the mosque. Not because it's unusual to find mosques and churches in close proximity—it's actually quite common in the secular states of the Levant—but because there are two churches in such a small residential area. Only 2 percent of Jordan's population is Christian, while 97 percent are Muslim.

I, meanwhile, am neither, and have plodded through the main entrance of the mosque with a hijab covering my head, without knowing that there is a separate entrance for non-Muslim tourists where you can pay two Jordanian dinars—about three US dollars—to get in. Consequently, I now have a hot-tempered man in a gray tunic in front of me, accusing me of trying to sneak in.

"Did you or did you not know that you have to pay?" he asks for the third time.

"No, I didn't know," I repeat.

The man looks skeptically at me, and the book I have under my arm. *The Meaning of the Holy Qu'ran*, a translated edition of the Quran by Abdullah Yusuf Ali. The gold-plated script shines at him in the sun.

"Are you a non-Muslim, a bad Muslim, or someone trying to sneak in without paying?" he asks.

I think of the options. None of them seems like a particularly good answer.

"I'm none of those," I answer. "I didn't know you have to pay."

"Why do you wear a hijab if you're not Muslim?"

I think about this, not knowing how to answer. It's a question I've asked myself many times before. I suppose the most honest explanation is that I wear the hijab in certain areas of town to avoid negative attention and to disappear into the crowd more easily, and also when I'm going into religious buildings. I've often wondered what Muslims think of people like me—people who wear hijabs without a theological motive. I ask the man if it's wrong of me to wear a hijab if I'm not a believer.

"No," he answers quickly. "It's a free country. You can dress in whatever you want." He looks at my book again. "Why are you reading that? The Quran must be read in Arabic."

I've also gotten this question several times, and thought a lot about it. A translation of the Quran is theologically problematic because the Holy Book cannot actually be translated. According to the Quran, Muhammad received his revelations in Arabic, and the text, with its multifaceted formulations and unique rhythms, cannot be reproduced in another language. Theologians emphasize that the Quran is identical to a sacred book that God possesses. In other words, it is God Himself who is speaking in the Quran, and the language is therefore closely connected to revelation. A translation therefore does not have sacred status—and can only be viewed as an interpretation. It's like a brand-new book when it has been translated. This thinking is in contrast with the Bible, which is viewed as a sacred text no matter what language it has been translated into.

"I don't speak Arabic well enough to read the Quran, but I still want to understand the Holy Book's message," I answer in an attempt to be politically correct.

"This Abdullah Yusuf Ali, is he an American?" the man asks, wrinkling his forehead suspiciously. He reaches out to take the book.

I hand it to him and tell him that Ali was a half-Indian, half-British Islamic scholar who could recite the whole Quran from memory. His translation is the most recognized in the English-speaking world, which is why I've chosen this interpretation.

The response seems to impress the man, since he smiles and says that he hopes that one day, *inshallah*—God willing—I will be able to read the Quran in the original language. I don't have to pay since I'm here looking for something bigger, he concludes, and wishes me a warm welcome.

I thank him for the hospitality and ask if he can perhaps show me around. His face lights up, and he agrees enthusiastically. He takes me along the white walls on the outside of the dome, where various inscriptions from the Quran have been written out in blue mosaic. He shows me where the women's hall is—a room with space enough for six hundred women, tiny in comparison with the neighboring room which has space for seven thousand men. He tells me that this is actually the only mosque in Amman that is open to tourists. Even though I'm a woman, I can visit the men's hall, he says, and lets me peek through the door. The room is decorated with an enormous chandelier and a colorful carpet adorned with red, blue, and gold patterns. The inside of the magnificent dome is embellished with stripes of blue and gold. A dozen men are sitting on the carpet facing Mecca. We move slowly past.

The man asks what has brought me to the Blue Mosque. I say that I've arranged to meet an imam here who is going to explain some of the verses of the Quran that I don't understand. I tell him I'm working on a book, and that the Quran is a central part of the text. The man grows skeptical again.

"You musn't reproduce the Quran directly," he says.

"Here in Jordan, a poet was arrested because he incorporated verses from the Quran in his poems."

I stare at him in astonishment. Even more unwritten rules! Is there a set of rules somewhere I can read up on? A book of what is right and wrong? I then realize that I'm probably holding it in my hand.

"Is it written in the Quran that the Quran shouldn't be directly quoted anywhere else?"

"In the Quran, yes," he replies, shrugging his shoulders. "Or hadith. Maybe one of the interpretations. The Constitution. I don't know. Just be careful."

I promise him I will and thank him for showing me around.

He says that I'm welcome to come back anytime and that I can stay as long as I'd like. He shuffles silently across the stone floor in his soft leather sandals and disappears around the corner of the mosque. I sit down in the shadow of the dome and leaf through the pages I've been told are about homosexuality. Three pink sticky notes mark the relevant *surahs* where the theme is dealt with.

The first sticky note marks Lot's story—the one Amina told me about—in which stones rained upon the residents of Sodom as punishment for their sins. The story is written in *surah* 11, which is called *Hud*, and depicts sodomy, which in Latin is actually referring directly to the city of Sodom and Lot's story and which in Christianity is called "the sin of Sodom." In Arabic, there isn't a literal reference to the word *sodomy* but rather "what Lot's people practiced"—that is, all forms of sexual intercourse that are forbidden according to the Quran.

For my own part, I agree with Amina's conclusions that the text has little to do with love between two people of the same gender, and that the content itself can be

interpreted in several ways. But the next *surah* I've marked—
surah 7, Al-A'raf (The Heights)—is very clearly talking
about homosexuality. There, in verses 80–81, it reads:

> And [We had sent] Lot when he said to his people,
> "Do you commit such immorality as no one has pre-
> ceded you with from among the worlds? Indeed, you
> approach men with desire, instead of women. Rather,
> you are a transgressing people."

Some scholars argue that this verse confirms that homosexuality is different (and worse) than other sins in the Quran.
If you read the text literally, the Arabic word used for the
sin the people committed means "obscene," "unnatural,"
and "pornographic," while other sexual sins in the Quran
(such as infidelity, incest, and pedophilia) are referred to as
sins of a more "normal" type.

I leaf through the book a bit further. The last sticky note
marks *surah 4, An-Nisa* (The Women), which deals with
the relationship between faith, remorse, and forgiveness,
shown through stories about how non-believers be-haved
when it came to God's warnings and messengers. It was
verses 17–18 that Amina had hoped her mother would recall
that morning she decided to tell her the truth. It reads:

> The repentance accepted by Allah is only for those
> who do wrong in ignorance [or carelessness] and then
> repent soon after. It is those to whom Allah will turn
> in forgiveness, and Allah is ever Knowing and Wise.

But repentance is not [accepted] of those who [con-
tinue to] do evil deeds up until, when death comes
to one of them, he says, "Indeed, I have repented
now," or of those who die while they are disbelievers.
For them We have prepared a painful punishment.

In Amina's interpretation, this verse meant that everyone
should get the chance to repent and change after being
warned, but her mother believed it was already too late—that
Aisha should be punished because her sins were so serious.

Besides *surahs* 11 and 7, I find little about homosexuality
in the Quran. This surprises me, since most conservative
Jordanians usually refer to an immense body of material
when they argue against homosexuality. I found it difficult to understand where these negative attitudes come
from until I realized there are a number of references to
homosexuality in the various hadiths. In this collection
of traditions, including sayings from the Prophet, homosexuality is referred to as a sin only people with perverse
instincts—and a total lack of shame and honor—are willing to do. According to the text, just the thought of the
punishment Allah would wreak upon those who carried
out this kind of sin got "heaven, earth, and mountains
to tremble." In one of the hadith, it is also stated, "The
Prophet (PBUH) has said: 'There is nothing that I fear more
for my *ummah* (nation) than the deed of the people of Lot.'"

So the text is quite clear to those who read it literally.
Since hadith is used as a guiding narrative about how to

best practice and live in line with the Quran and Islam, it's no wonder that homosexuality is viewed as a serious sin in more conservative environments.

I close the Quran and look out over the open square. A young woman with a pink hijab, black wool jacket, and childlike smile walks between the tall pillars at the entrance. She comes toward me, waves, and introduces herself. Her name is Sameeha, she's sixteen and the imam's daughter. She's come to take me to their house, which is next door to the mosque. I get up and follow her. She leads me be-neath the white pillars that surround the big square, out of the mosque itself, and into their house, where I'm asked to sit and wait for her father. I sit on the floral-patterned pale yellow sofa and look around the room, which has bookshelves from floor to ceiling filled with Arabic books and texts.

"Welcome," says a voice I've already heard calling speeches from the prayer towers over Amman. I look up at the imam. He has a short, dark beard, looks like he's in his forties, and is wearing a dark-brown floor-length tunic and a luxurious-looking cloak. He smiles and sits on the couch across from me. He tells me he's very happy about my inquiry.

"It's not every day an internationally known journalist contacts me to inquire about theological questions," he says.

I thank him for the recognition but point out that I'm not exactly an internationally known journalist, even though I've written quite a bit from Jordan.

"Well, I'm not exactly an internationally known imam either," he jokes. He turns to face me. "So, are you a believer?"

I shake my head and tell him that I was baptized and confirmed in the Church of Norway but that I'm not particularly religious.

"But you've read the Bible, and perhaps recognize many of the stories you found in the Quran?"

I think about this. It's probably been twenty years since I last read the Bible. It must have been sometime in elementary school when we read about Moses, Noah, and the disciples. Even though it was a long time ago, and the stories in the Bible are written more like a narrative whereas the ones in the Quran are almost like repeated simple statements from Allah, I do recognize many of the same themes and characters. The accounts of Adam, David, Abraham, Moses, Noah, Jesus, and Mary are in both books.

"I haven't read much of the Quran or the Bible," I admit.

He says that I seemed well-read when I asked him so specifically about the story of Lot. "You find this story both in the Quran and the Old Testament," he says. He explains that the texts are almost identical: both stories tell of Lot and his family who had to flee from Sodom. As they left, his wife looked back, which led to her turning into a pillar of salt. Lot and his two daughters then fled into the mountains above the Jordan Valley. In the Bible, the two daughters get Lot drunk on wine and have sex with him when he falls asleep. They both get pregnant and give birth to children who are the original fathers of the families of Moab and Ammon. This part about Lot's daughters lying with him is not mentioned in the Quran. There, Lot is considered to be a prophet and it is therefore unlikely that he'll be accused of things like incest. Nevertheless, the main message of the stories about Lot in the Bible and in the Quran is the same: they are both about sodomy.

I ponder what the imam has said, thinking that it seems unlikely that God saves Lot and wipes out an entire people because of sodomy only to let him commit the same sin again. In any case, there is little in the story that points to love between two people of the same gender—which is the reason that I wanted to speak with the imam in the first place.

"Where in the Quran does it say it's forbidden to love someone of the same gender?" I ask.

"That's simple. The Holy Quran forbids sex outside marriage. There are clear rules about who can enter a marriage; it's a relationship reserved for man and woman. And if someone isn't married and has sex, it is *haram*. So it's clear that homosexuality is forbidden."

I can't come up with any good counterarguments. Like conservative Christians, conservative Muslims claim that homosexuality is forbidden based on a literal interpretation of the text. The Jordanian penal code, however, had already decriminalized homosexuality by 1951, thereby taking a step in a more liberal direction.

"But homosexuality isn't forbidden in Jordan, even though Islam is the state religion?" I note, and am excited to hear what he thinks about this.

"There's no incompatibility in it," he says, explaining that the Jordanian Constitution states that Islam is the country's state religion, but also that the country has one court for religious cases and another for civil matters. Sharia and the penal code are practiced side by side in Jordanian society. The religious courts settle matters of family law (including honor, blood money, and inheritance) based on Islamic or Christian religious laws. The civil courts, in contrast, judge legal questions that aren't covered by the religious laws.

I think about this. The way I understand it, the penal code must have little significance as cases of homosexuality as these cases are to be evaluated by one of the religious courts, according to the Constitution. For the 97 percent of the Jordanian population who are Muslims, the case will be settled per sharia, which clearly says that homosexuality is forbidden—and an acceptable reason to kill someone for honor.

"But that doesn't make any sense. How can homosexuality be legal according to the penal code but illegal in practice?" I ask, not fully understanding. This example illustrates just how contradictory the Jordanian legal system can be, and how easy it is for the authorities to use the rules to preserve the country's conservative attitudes without attracting any attention internationally. Because on paper there are no clauses in Jordanian law that criminalize or discriminate against homosexuality—but when the rules are challenged in practice, homosexuality is deemed to be undesirable and illegal.

For example, the Minister of the Interior published a statement claiming that LGBT groups were illegal after Jordan was pushed to legalize gay marriage in 2015. He justified the statement by claiming that the Jordanian state respects Islam and sharia, and that the legalization of LGBT groups is in violation with these—and therefore also the Jordanian Constitution—which makes it illegal. In order to make the message clear, he wrote, "Any proposition from the 'sexually perverse' that contradicts the basis of sharia and normal law and order is prohibited."

The reference to the Constitution stating that Islam is the state religion in Jordan—and that Islam forbids homosexuality, which also indirectly makes homosexuality illegal according to the penal code—clearly shows how the legal system safeguards controversial attitudes without having to take responsibility for them directly. The legislation is inconsistent and reflects the contradictions that exist between modernity and tradition in the country. The same paradox exists between international law, which Jordan has signed, and national legislation. For example, Jordan ratified the Convention on the Elimination of All Forms of Discrimination Against Women (CEDAW, or the Women's Convention) but made exceptions for certain controversial articles. In practice, *Jordanian* law is ultimately legally binding if two laws oppose each other.

"Homosexuality is undesirable. But it shouldn't be punishable by death," says the imam, explaining that the Jordanian penal code no longer allows family members to beat or kill one of their own relatives because their sexuality brings shame to the family. The jurisprudence that is practiced in Jordan belongs to the Hanafi school of thought. This interpretation of sharia is considered to be the most liberal of the four schools of law recognized by

Sunni Muslims. The Hanafi school doesn't approve of the death penalty for homosexuality, on the basis of a hadith that states that "Muslim blood should not spill" for reasons other than adultery, apostasy, or murder. This is in stark contrast with the Hanbali school of thought, which interprets sodomy as a form of adultery and therefore believes that it should be punishable by death. It is each school of thought's attitudes and interpretations about what is right and wrong that underlies national legislation in the different Islamic countries.

"In fact, it became illegal to kill someone in the name of honor in Jordan in 2013, whatever the reason may be." He raises his eyebrows, as though this information should impress me.

But I'm not impressed. I know that the amendment he is referring to is article 341, which in 2013 went from stating that "murder is legal as long as the person who kills or harms another person does it to defend their own life or their own honor" to "a husband or close relative who kills a woman in a situation where there is a particular reason to suspect that she has been unfaithful shall be pardoned with a reduced punishment."

While the text has changed in theory, little has changed in practice. If the family forgives the person who has done the killing and the killer says that the crime was carried out in a state of passion, the punishment is minimal.

In a way, the legislation opens itself to interpretation when it comes to what is right and wrong. As long as the state pardons those who commit honor killings, many families will take matters into their own hands. Thus, the Jordanian state balances the legislation on a very thin line between the liberal and the most conservative attitudes in the country—without the government having to take a clear stance.

When all is said and done, the attitudes of Jordanian society and the family's point of view about the case determine how someone is punished. There is also a broad consensus in Jordan today that homosexuality is undesirable and that honor killing is acceptable in certain situations.

"What do *you* think, as an imam and a religious leader, about people killing in the name of honor in this country?"

The imam shakes his head and looks sad. "People who do such things aren't living in line with the Quran. They don't understand the Holy Book. All the problems we Muslims face today are due to such misinterpretations."

I agree with him, and ask what can be done to prevent honor killings in a country like Jordan.

"When it comes to honor, people are willing to do anything to protect their own reputation. It has nothing to do with Islam. That's why the mufti has just issued a fatwa that forbids honor killing."

I'm pleasantly surprised to hear this. A fatwa is a legal assessment of what complies with Islamic law. It isn't legally binding but informs and expresses an opinion from a scholar. A fatwa is a strong signal that can be used actively as a counterargument for those who still justify these actions through Islam.

For the first time since I started researching honor killings, I see an attempt to prevent these crimes that I actually believe can improve the situation in Jordan.

"That's fantastic," I say.

The imam nods, looks at the clock, and apologizes. He says that we must end the interview now if he is to make it to the calls from the tower.

I smile, and follow him and his daughter out toward the mosque.

"Read the Quran at your own pace. And come back if there is anything you are wondering about!" he shouts as he runs across the big square to make it to his prayers on time.

Shortly after, I hear the sound of his voice ringing out over the city, promising God's forgiveness, mercy, and love. It is so beautiful that the atheist in me almost wants to cover my ears. Honor killing has nothing to do with Islam, I think. And as long as the practice isn't rooted in religion, there is always hope for change.

***

THEY'D BEEN WAITING outside of Maram's house for over an hour. It was a chilly evening and Amina was impatient—and worried that her mother and Baba would find out that they'd come here. She looked at Aisha. She could almost see her heart beating beneath her sweater.

"Do it now," she whispered again, indicating that Aisha should throw the stone at Maram's window and get her to come down to say goodbye—for good. She had to be responsible for what she had done and face the consequences of the choices she had made.

Aisha nodded and shut her eyes, took a deep breath, and pulled a stone from her pocket. It was a smooth black stone. She clenched her fist around it and flopped her hand down against her body as though this little rock were so heavy that her arm didn't even have the power to lift the weight.

Aisha had told Amina that she and Maram had been doing this almost every week for a few months now. They had stood outside one another's houses, throwing pebbles at each other's windows. They had snuck out together and taken long walks through the dark streets in the evenings. Sometimes Aisha had stood outside for hours, staring up at Maram's window and waiting for the lights in all the other rooms to be turned off, almost bursting with excitement. The time she spent with Maram was the only thing that meant anything to her.

Their romance had been reserved for the nighttime, hidden by the darkness of the graves and in the parks. Their love had grown between tombstones and weeds.

They went on walks, held hands, whispered compliments, and talked about their dreams as they stared into one another's eyes. Maram was the only thing Aisha thought about all day. The only thing she wanted. The only thing she longed for. The days passed dreaming about the evenings. The light was only a reminder of the darkness she longed for so much.

Neither of them had ever dared to steal a first kiss—before that time at the beach house when Amina had seen them, and their romance suddenly had to come to an end.

Aisha was convinced that she would never be happy without Maram, but Amina knew better. She promised that this feeling would pass—and besides, Aisha didn't have any choice. She and Maram had to completely cut off contact—and they had. They had stayed away from each other for several weeks now, but Aisha refused to live unless she got to say a proper goodbye. Heartbreak had poisoned her thoughts. She had threatened to take her mother's advice, to buy some pills from the pharmacy and take her own life. Amina understood that perhaps a last meeting had to take place for Aisha to be able to move on—which was why she had come with her today, so that their parents wouldn't grow suspicious. So that Aisha could say a proper goodbye, one last time.

Aisha took a breath, raised her arm, and threw the stone at the window on the second floor. She stood there looking upwards. Her throat quivered. Then she pulled another stone from her pocket and threw it, hitting the glass so it clattered. She threw three, four, five more stones. A shadow appeared in the darkened room and the window opened carefully. Aisha grinned broadly and put her hand over her heart. Maram smiled back. She stretched out three fingers to show that she would be right down.

Aisha bowed her head and paced back and forth impatiently. She picked up the stones she had thrown and put them back into her pocket.

"Come," she said to Amina, walking quickly down the dark alley that led to the house and up a narrow path to a backyard where no one could see them. "You can keep watch here," she said, pointing at the top of the path.

Amina squatted obediently beside a ramshackle stone wall while Aisha continued into the backyard toward an enormous oak tree. Amina looked at her with a lump in her throat, watching as Aisha sat beneath the tree, rested her arms on her knees, and laid her head in her hands. Aisha pulled off her hijab. It was clear that she was in pain, but there was no other way. Their mother would kill them if Aisha and Maram kept seeing each other—they were both convinced of that. There was no other alternative.

Maram came walking down the path. She disappeared past Amina as if she didn't even see her sitting there. She ran toward Aisha, who got up and threw her arms around her. Aisha squeezed her eyes shut, and her body seemed to collapse as they held each other. She buried her head in Maram's wavy hair. Maram's back rose and fell to the sound of deep sobs. Amina looked away.

"I am so incredibly sorry," she heard Maram say. It seemed like Aisha couldn't get out a single word. The only thing that Amina could hear was her sobbing.

She looked at the two of them. Couldn't they just get it over with and say goodbye? Soon, Baba and Mamma would start to wonder where they'd gone.

Aisha clung to Maram, and kissed her cheek with trembling lips. Then she leaned forward and kissed her on the mouth.

Amina cleared her throat loudly. This was not a part of the agreement. She would never witness her sister sinning again without intervening.

"We're leaving now, Aisha," she said sternly, walking toward them. "Let go of my sister, Maram. Don't you see you're going to kill her?"

Maram stared at Amina, clinging to Aisha with trembling hands before letting go and stroking her fingertips over her wet cheeks.

"She's right," said Maram, pushing Aisha away firmly. "You came to say goodbye. I understand. And I respect it."

Aisha didn't respond. She just shut her eyes and bit her lip. Amina took her hand and pulled her behind her, up the path. Aisha didn't protest. She just stumbled along without looking back. She sobbed loudly and let the tears fall. They walked a few blocks before she collapsed, grabbed her stomach, and threw up. She got up and clung to Amina, just as she had been clinging to Maram. Amina stroked her back and dried her cheeks with the sleeve of her jacket. She promised yet again that this would pass, that the worst was over now, that Allah was testing her but that she had won. Aisha held her hands in front of her mouth to hold back the sobs.

"I can still smell her perfume, Amina. It's all I have left of her. Smell." Aisha stretched her hands out.

Amina looked at Aisha sternly. "From now on, we never speak of Maram, okay? She doesn't exist. Never existed. You're dead to her, and she's dead to you. This way we can all survive!"

Aisha nodded mechanically. She wiped away the rest of the mascara that had collected beneath her eyes. She got up, taking a few wobbly steps before she could collect herself and start breathing normally. She put her hijab back in place and straightened up. Her gaze was more determined than it had been in a long time.

"But you're wrong, Amina," she said at last. "It isn't Maram who's killing me. It's you."

Amina looked away. She didn't know how to respond. Aisha was wrong, she thought. She had *saved her*. One day, she would understand and thank her when this sinful little crush had passed.

They walked the rest of the way home in silence, looking over the mountaintops that sparkled in the light of the streetlamps in the dark night, then up at the empty night sky.

When they got home, Akram met them in the hallway and asked where they'd been. Amina said they had been out for a walk. He looked at them skeptically.

"Tell me where you've been," he said.

Amina snorted and said it was none of his business. Why was he wondering anyway, she asked.

"Do you think I don't know what you're up to?"

Amina shook her head. "Stop spying on us, Akram. You aren't our father," she said, shaking her head and disappearing into their room.

"I know that you met her!" he shouted after them. "I'm going to tell Baba!"

***

"JUST ONE KISS! One little kiss!"

The cars are honking at me and loud compliments in Arabic are shouted at me from the open windows. I'm standing along the main road in one of Amman's most trafficked intersections waiting to meet one of my friends from the neighboring city of Irbid. After two years of research in the country, I've made several friends who are constantly inviting me to social gatherings in the evenings. It's usually dinner with their families, movies, debates, or house parties I'm invited to, but this time they've asked me out on the town.

I feel extraordinarily insecure but am trying to convince myself that the attention isn't intended maliciously. I'm a single woman out after nine at night in a traditional neighborhood, so it's not strange that passersby are reacting. As a rule, when I go out in Amman after dark, I wear a hijab and a long jacket, but today I'm just wearing jeans and a sweater, with my hair down. In a way, I'm asking for this attention, I think, and it's nice to see that I am treated somewhat normally as long as I respect the culture and dress as it's expected here.

A message pops up on my phone. "Go to the pub down the street and meet us there," Samir writes. I look down the road skeptically and realize that it's probably just as morally incorrect for me to stand outside alone as a woman as it is to sit in a bar.

When he invited me earlier that evening, Samir tried to convince me that no one would look down at me if I went out in Amman but I'm skeptical nonetheless. All the attention from the passing cars just supported my prejudices that a woman who goes out alone in Amman will be judged negatively and condemned by society.

I walk determinedly down the steep road that goes past the bar and notice an older regular sitting outside, looking at me. I know his face well, and he definitely also recognizes me. This is the part of town I usually stay in when I visit Amman, and most people have likely figured out who I am. The rumor mill in Amman is extremely effective; most people hear when someone moves in or out of their neighborhood, and everything that happens is a topic for debate.

The area I live in is right between the modern and traditional parts of the city. At the top of the hill is the Jabal Al-Wiebdeh neighborhood with its organic cafes, hipster locals, and colorful art galleries, while down here closer to Abdali, it's mostly burka-clad women, small hairdressers, kiosk vendors, and traders who fill the streets. Amman is like this: an assemblage of different environments and social circles that are sometimes highly contradictory—which makes it difficult to grasp what the *real* culture of the city is. What is acceptable in one neighborhood or group can be completely unthinkable for another just a few streets away.

I imagine how the gossip will be in this little neighborhood if they hear that I've been out after nine and drunk alcohol with a man I'm not related to. At the top of the hill such evening activities are acceptable, but down here they will certainly judge me.

"*Norwiji!*" the regular shouts, clapping his hands when he realizes that I am actually thinking about going into the bar this time. I say hello, but enter without starting a conversation.

My first impression of the place is surprisingly positive. A dozen people—mostly men in their thirties—are sitting with beers in front of them, chatting with each other. Their voices are relaxed, the interior is dark wood, and the speakers in the corners of the room are emitting a kind of Arabic attempt at rock—which quickly gets me feeling like I could be back in any pub in Europe. I sit down at an empty table and order a beer from the man behind the bar. He smiles, fills a glass, and places a bowl of warm nuts in front of me. I regard those around me curiously. I'm the only woman here but it seems to be fine, I think. Maybe Samir is right after all.

Shortly after, Samir struts through the door with two friends and a woman with uncovered bleached hair. She is wearing eyeliner and dark red lipstick, and I am immediately struck by her beauty. The two other friends are well dressed in tight pants and light shirts and have perfectly groomed eyebrows and freshly trimmed beards. If I didn't know any better I'd have guessed a group of models had just entered the room. Samir himself is tall and dark with a medium-length beard, green eyes, and a big smile. He is undoubtedly a handsome man with a lot of charisma—which was why I started talking to him when I was out a few weeks ago. We exchanged numbers and stayed in touch, and have become good friends during the short time we've known each other.

The gang surrounds me, shaking my hand and giving me long hugs. Samir says we're going to drink *arak*, a strong liquor with an alcohol content of up to 60 percent. I grimace skeptically, and Samir pats me carefully on the shoulder.

"You'll be fine," he says, laughing. "You're a Viking!"

"Arak!" cries out the friend who introduced himself as Ali. Shortly thereafter, an enormous bottle with blue writing is placed on the table along with five narrow glasses and two pints of water. Ali mixes the liquor with the water in the small glasses, and the liquid turns into a cloudy, milky substance. I'm getting the chills just looking at it, and even a bit nauseous from the sweet smell of anise that meets my nose as I take the drink.

"*Nnakhbak*—to health," says Ali, and we all raise our glasses.

"*Skål*—cheers," I respond and knock back the liquid that tastes a lot like cough syrup.

The hours pass quickly, and the bottle is soon empty. We eat mezze and indulge in freshly baked Arabic bread that we dip in hummus, baba ghanoush, and labneh—a dip that resembles a cross between feta and cream. Labneh is definitely my favorite, and I eat so much that my stomach starts to hurt. The conversation flows and the mood rises as we continue drinking. Samir says he wants to go out to a club, while Ali would prefer to drive around town and listen to music in the car. On Saturday nights, the streets of Amman are packed with cars full of friends, alcohol, and loud music. In Norway, I would perhaps have called them hooligans, but here the practice has a slightly different social function, as it's the easiest way for young people to meet. Hidden in their own cars, men and women can be out on the town together, drink, and get to know one another—without being exposed to the critical gaze of the outside world.

The woman, Mary, says she'd rather go out since there's so much traffic. They've already been sitting in the car from Irbid for an hour and a half anyway, she points out. I say I can go along with whatever they decide. I'm not so familiar with Amman's nightlife and just want to see what they want to do.

"We're going to Books@cafe," Samir says.

"Books@cafe?" I ask, surprised. It's the only place I actually *do* know of in Amman; it's known for being a meeting place for the LGBT community. Samir blinks and pours another round of arak, proposing yet another *cheers*— without mixing the alcohol with water this time.

"To tonight!" he shouts, knocking back the drink and leaning toward me. He whispers that he likes both women and men.

I throw back my own drink and don't know how to react. Then I stare at Ali in his tight shirt and with his perfectly groomed eyebrows.

"Do you know what kind of place it is?" Mary asks, and it grows quiet around the table. Everyone looks at me.

I nod, still uncertain about how to act. Could it just be a coincidence that my closest new friend here in Amman is bi, or is he here to lure me into a trap? I go over the facts in my head. On paper, it's not illegal to be homosexual in Jordan, and I've never read any cases of tourists being prosecuted or convicted for being openly gay in the country. Even though homosexuality is considered sinful behavior, it is a private matter that the state mostly doesn't get involved in. The family deals with the "issue" internally, and different families choose different solutions. The authorities can't kick me out even if they have evidence that I'm gay, I conclude. Besides, I was the one who introduced myself to Samir when we first met, not the other way around, so the friendship seems genuine.

"I've been there before," I admit.

"I KNEW it!" shouts Mary, clapping her hands enthusiastically. "You're one of us."

I look at the group in front of me and start laughing. The thought hadn't struck me, but now it is obvious. The tight jeans and shirt Ali is wearing suddenly have a logical explanation, as do Samir's delicate handshakes and the way his two friends are acting with each other. Stereotypes, maybe, but also facts in this case.

"Maybe," I say. "Are you all gay?"

The group erupts into laughter.

"Yes!" Mary says, ordering another round, and the mood rises further. "Let's celebrate!"

"But I'm not gay," Samir corrects eventually. "I just have sex with men. And I'm masculine. No one is *really* gay in Amman. Here, you're bi, not gay."

I ask what he means by that, and he explains that he thinks it's okay to have sex with someone of the same gender but that it isn't okay to live in an open lesbian or gay relationship.

"That would be selfish," he says. "It would be hard for the family."

"Would they kill you if they found out?" I ask.

He grins and says no. Jordan isn't a primitive country where barbaric Arabic men kill their children before breakfast, he remarks.

I think about this comment for a while. In a way, he's both right and wrong. After all, there are about twenty men who kill their children in the name of honor in this country every year, including for reasons such as this. But, like homosexuals in this country, they only represent a small subculture, a minority. Neither gays nor those who kill in the name of honor represent the majority in this country. I realize that I have been focusing only on two extremes of Jordanian society. For months, I have examined the darkest sides of the culture, looking for oppression, prejudice, and murder... but there are of course also parts of Jordan where people can more freely love whomever they want and be more open about their sexuality. Honor killing is an ancient cultural phenomenon founded on its own form of logic, and it is increasingly taking place in societies where modern values are gaining traction. It's only at the extremes that things go wrong. This is an important nuance, I think, and empty my last glass of arak.

"How does it really work, concealing your sexuality?" I ask, wondering if the family won't find out eventually anyway when they never get married.

"I'm going to marry a woman, get a good job, a house, kids. Like I said, I'm not gay." Samir hits his chest.

Mary leans forward and tells me that there are many ways of solving this issue in Jordan. Sometimes, gay people search for other gay people of the opposite gender with whom they can build a family. They share a home, have children, and live just like any other family—but they are also living a double life on the side with other partners. This way, you can both meet your family's expectations and live the life you want.

"Doesn't it feel like living a lie?" I ask.

"You just have to be considerate," she says. "You always have a choice between yourself and your family. Just like we cover up our women with veils, we cover up our secrets. As long as we hide our sins from the public, it's fine."

Her perspective surprises me. And as we tumble out of the bar and drive toward Al-Rainbow Street in the humid summer night, I feel more out of place and illegal in this country than I have in a long time. My like-minded friends think that what they're doing is a sin. They have given up the right to their own sexuality and are living a double life in which they are neither faithful to themselves nor to society's norms.

* * *

HER HEART ALMOST stopped each time Amina looked over at Aisha's empty bed. Days had turned into weeks. Weeks into months. She still wondered if they'd done the right thing. She still considered whether Baba could ever actually take the lives of his own children. Was he— their dear father, who had always protected them and taken care of them—truly capable of killing one of his own?

She remembered the conversation she and Baba had had in the desert. He had suggested that he was a victim of societal values when he killed his own mother, as though he hadn't had any other choice. That it wasn't his fault that his mother died, since there were others demanding him to kill her. Amina pondered this: wasn't a man who killed for something he really believed in better than a man who killed quite simply because he didn't dare do otherwise? Baba thought he was innocent because society's demands were stronger than his individual responsibility, and a person who doesn't recognize his fault for something he regrets could very well do the same thing again, couldn't he?

Yes, he *could* kill his own children, Amina thought. At least, that was what she had concluded the evening she decided to tell Aisha everything.

"I'm afraid Baba will kill you," she had said straight out, and told Aisha what she knew about Baba's past.

Aisha was terrified. She lost her appetite, couldn't sleep, vomited for the first few evenings. A week later, she woke Amina in the middle of the night and told her she felt like her heart was going to burst from her chest. She said her hands and feet were numb.

Amina didn't know what to do other than lie down in the bed next to Aisha and hold her until she fell asleep several hours later. She lay awake herself, listening to Aisha's breath, fearing that it would suddenly stop.

The night after was even worse. Aisha had trouble breathing. She clawed at her throat and gasped for air; it looked like she was being suffocated and Amina couldn't calm her down this time. Aisha's eyes rolled backwards and her body went into spasms. Horrified, Amina pulled Aisha into the bathroom and dunked her head in ice-cold water. She slapped her face to try to wake her up again. Confused, Aisha slowly came around. The experience scared them both. It was their first encounter with a panic attack—one of many over the next weeks.

One night several days later, as Amina was sitting awake for the third night in a row watching Aisha's back heaving as she gagged over the toilet bowl, she realized something had to be done.

"It's worse than before," Aisha said before new convulsions overcame her and she almost couldn't manage to speak anymore. "We have to go to the hospital."

Amina didn't know how to answer. If they went to the hospital, they would have to tell the doctor what was wrong and involve other people in an issue that only concerned their family. If they didn't go, however, she wasn't sure what would happen. She had never seen Aisha so sick and weak before.

Aisha threw up again before she leaned back with bloodshot eyes and took a deep, rattling breath. "I can't live here any longer, Amina!" she said. "I need to get away."

Amina sank down next to her on the bathroom floor. She shook at the thought of what was about to happen. If Aisha left or asked the authorities for help, it would be like publicly accusing Baba of wanting to kill them. Would they really accuse their own father of being a murderer? What if they were wrong? What if Baba had changed?

Still, she knew Aisha was right. She couldn't live this way anymore. They couldn't risk her life. She needed to leave. They had no other choice.

"It's so unfair that something that happened over such a short time could change an entire life," Amina said to Aisha.

"I feel like that time was worth an entire life," Aisha replied.

Amina started to tear up. How could her sister say such a thing? It was heartbreakingly, painfully honest. It was the truth about a kind of love that turned out to be something else—something selfish. Something cynical. For a while Amina could only sit there, grieving that her family was about to be shattered, that Baba would be accused of being a killer, and that they would probably have to break contact as sisters, but Aisha didn't regret anything at all. On the contrary, she would have done the same thing again. She would sacrifice everyone who loved her for someone she had barely known for a few months.

Amina sat next to Aisha in silence. This was the beginning of the end, she realized, and felt like she was dissociating from her body. In a flash, she was sitting in the bathroom next to Aisha and was six years old, maybe a bit older. They had painted their nails in all the colors of the rainbow and covered their lips with their mother's dark red lipstick. They were pretending they were dressing up for all of the holy festivals and special occasions—'Eid Al-Fitr after Ramadan, 'Eid Al-Adha after the pilgrimage, weddings, births.

She then bounced back to the present through a kind of strange passage between what had been and what would no longer be. To a lost future. Aisha didn't regret what she had done. She had been warned but still didn't want to change. She was different from the person Amina had always loved. Amina felt an almost violent alienation growing between them. Her love for her sister and her grief fought against her feelings, and she didn't know if she should be angry, indifferent, or sad. She tried to think rationally.

"I understand," she said at last.

They agreed to find a solution, but there weren't many alternatives. Aisha couldn't move to another city. She needed money, a job, and a husband. And besides, Baba or their uncles would find her no matter where in Jordan she went, and then they would most certainly kill her. She couldn't leave Jordan either. They had no money, no passports, and no contacts. They mulled over the matter for hours but couldn't come up with any good solution.

"Let's just go to the hospital," Aisha said in the end, dizzy with anxiety and exhaustion. "I just want to be able to breathe normally."

Amina wrapped her arms around her and kissed her on the forehead three times. Perhaps the doctors could give her something to help with the panic attacks, or even protect her. Perhaps they could send her on to a specialist who could help her with the feelings she had for Maram. She whispered calmly that everything would be better soon, stroked Aisha's hair, and hugged her tightly. Amina helped her up and they packed up some of her clothes, a toothbrush, and makeup in a bag. She also added her mother's red-flowered hijab they were always fighting over. She didn't know why, but it just felt right that Aisha should have it now.

Then they disappeared into the night. They closed the front door silently without locking it so Amina could return before the morning light revealed that Aisha had gone.

***

I WAKE SHARPLY as the sun penetrates the room, striking me right in the eyes. For the last few weeks, I've been wandering indifferently around Amman's pale yellow streets, waiting for a response from the authorities; I've requested permission to visit the Jwaideh Women's Prison. I've filled out countless forms and stood in never-ending lines at all of the government's local offices—just to be sent from one city police station to another without my case seeming to move forward at all. I seem to have ended up in an inhospitable place in the Jordanian bureaucracy: in the midst of stiffly clad security guards and men in expensive suits who emphasize that I have the lowest priority in every queue—because I am a woman.

I think of the boss I need a signature from, who is most certainly nodding off in his office, nonchalantly drinking his Arabic coffee while the innocent women I'm trying to interview are trapped in jail.

I can't wait anymore and decide to go directly to his office to confront him. I want to look him right in the eyes.

Five hours and one sweaty taxi ride later, the irritation quickly transforms into nerves as I realize that the building for the Public Security Directorate—where the head boss has his office—looks like an enormous cross between the Taj Mahal and the Central Intelligence Agency's headquarters.

I'm stopped by a uniformed policeman who asks what I'm doing outside the ministry's offices, strutting freely between the enormous wall that surrounds the place and the barbed wire fence along the highway. I look up at the officer, who is tracing the lines of my face with a loaded AG3, and tell him I have a meeting with the boss.

He asks me how I've gotten here, forty minutes from town. On foot. I explain that the taxi driver wouldn't drive me all the way to the entrance, so he let me out farther down the road and I walked the rest of the way. I try my luck with a smile, and the man lowers his weapon.

"You can't just walk around here," he says. "No one just walks in here! Do you have any ID?"

I take out every piece of identification I have and give them to him. He leafs laboriously through my passport, page by page, as I squirm anxiously beside him. My hands are clammy and my armpits are dripping with sweat. I am wearing sandals and am suddenly aware that I am absolutely *not* dressed properly for a meeting at as strict a place as this one.

"Get in," he says finally, pointing his gun at the black Jeep he drove up in.

I follow him obediently and settle nervously into the back seat.

"Who are you?" he asks when we're both in the car. Both he and his colleague, who is driving, turn and look at me curiously.

I explain why I'm there, and that I'm going to speak to the head of the department. The two men look at their watches, then at me, then point out that it's four thirty.

"The boss has already gone for the day," says the police-man who first accosted me.

"But we've arranged a meeting," I say, hoping that the men can help me into this monster of a building and that the boss is still there.

"Yes, well then," says his colleague, and the car motors along the tall wall up toward the entrance. They are talk-ative and tell me they worked as ordinary policemen before they started as guards for the security department. They still have police authority, they say, and if I experience any-thing that makes me uncomfortable, I can just call them. They can do whatever they want, they tell me, and hand me two cards with Arabic writing. I thank them and ask whether, as "ordinary" policemen, they ever worked on a case involving honor killing.

"No, never," the guard says curtly. "It never happens. That kind of thing is handled within the family."

"Really?" I ask, thinking about what Amina told me in the desert, about how she wasn't allowed to leave even if she wanted to. "Isn't there any kind of law that prevents this kind of criminal behavior?"

"Yes," answers the driver. "I mean, there are rules to keep people from killing each other. But the authorities don't ever get involved in someone else's honor business."

"Plus, women have to be protected from their family," says the first officer. "And from themselves."

I don't say anything.

We reach the first checkpoint, where a guard is standing inside a little shack that is shading him from the blazing afternoon sun. The policeman speaks to him, shows him my passport, and the guard picks up the phone. He calls someone inside and says that a guest has come to visit. I hear him say my name and ID number.

"Who are you meeting?" he asks.

"The head of the Public Security Directorate," I reply.

He passes the message along, gets an answer from someone at the other end, looks at me nervously, and asks me to get out of the car.

"You're in," says the policeman, winking at me and wishing me good luck.

Well, that was easy, I think, and get out of the car. I'm standing in front of two enormous steel gates that cast long shadows over me. I cautiously poke my head inside and am guided by various guards who alternately smile and aim their weapons at me—seemingly randomly. I look up at the immense walls, which are made of white stones with carved details. Small ornamental shrubs are scattered across a green park that surrounds the entire building.

So this is where they sit when they are *not* answering my calls or letters, I think, desperately searching for some of the energy and aggression I woke up with earlier that day.

I walk across a very large square where there is yet another guard at the end who greets me. He follows me through what turns out to be the main entrance.

"Apologies, Madam," he says, explaining that we need to take a little detour because he doesn't have the keys to the door we should be using.

After having walked through a labyrinth of hallways, staircases, and large halls, we arrive at an office where a man with a dark moustache and a shiny bald head is sitting on the phone. He waves me in carelessly without even lifting his gaze. I can tell immediately that he is arrogant, and well aware of his own authority. I sit down in a burgundy leather chair that is strategically placed a foot and a half lower than his own chair—certainly to emphasize the fact that he has more power than his visitors. His office is full of all the garish leather interior decorations that seem to be so popular in Jordan.

The man puts down the phone and says his name is Maher. He asks who I am and what I want to talk to him about. He can't quite remember that we've arranged a meeting, but he has meetings with many people during a day and must apologize. I answer partly honestly, and tell him I sent a letter asking for permission to enter the women's prison—over three years ago. Then again two years ago. A year ago as well. Then a few months ago. And a week ago. I summarize that I have been badgering the directorate for more than three years by phone and email, in English and in Arabic, without getting any response.

"Well," Maher says, and pulls out my letter which seems, quite randomly, to be at the top of the pile of paper on his desk. "There's something missing," he says.

"Something missing?" I ask. He picks up the phone, ignoring my question, and calls someone as he reads what I've written on the sheet. I'm trying to understand what he is saying, but the conversation is going far too fast for my somewhat limited Arabic abilities. He leans back in his office chair and yawns.

"It's missing an email address," he says, with the phone up to his ear.

"It's not," I say, pointing at the top of the sheet where all the contact information is listed.

"It's missing a contact person," he says.

"That's me," I answer, and point at the section where I describe who I am and why I want to visit the prison.

Maher ends the call and punches in a new number. He's still avoiding looking me in the eyes. In fact, he's avoiding looking in my direction at all.

"I just need a proper answer," I say. "Just give me a yes or a no!"

Maher passes me the phone and tells me to explain who I am and what I want to a man at the other end of the line. I take the phone and explain that I'm a foreign journalist who wants to visit the Jwaideh Women's Prison because one of my interviewees spent a long part of her life there to avoid being killed by her family.

The stranger seems interested in what I'm saying, and says he agrees that this information is important and should come to light. He asks where and when the information will be published, and if I'm a well-known journalist, and when I've thought about returning to Norway.

It isn't until he asks if I've sent parts of what I've written to anyone outside Jordan yet that I realize I've voluntarily wandered right into the lion's den and am now sitting here like bloody beef tartare, ready to be stripped of everything

I've been working on for the last three years. It's clear that the authorities don't want this information to get out. International attention is undesirable in general, after all—at least if it regards such a negative and controversial topic.

"I've sent everything to a lot of people," I answer.

The stranger at the other end says he'd like to speak to Maher again. I hand over the phone and listen to half of the incomprehensible discussion between the two as the daylight slowly disappears outside.

A third person enters the room and asks for a copy of my passport. My visa is about to expire, he points out, and says that I have to take a blood test if I want to get it extended. I realize that this visit was definitely a bad idea. The authorities are going to follow everything I do from now on, which will make it harder to conduct interviews with Rahman and protect his identity as well as those of other interviewees I'm trying to meet.

"We would very much like to help you get into the prison," Maher says, and it's no longer easy to know if he would like to help me to get in there as a journalist—or an inmate.

"You will receive a reply from us within seventy-two hours," he adds, and I immediately understand that this is just another stop along the endless journey through the Jordanian bureaucracy. The permission I need will never appear because the answer is no. But they won't hold themselves responsible for that. Because a no requires an explanation, which they clearly lack. That's likely why they're delaying my case.

I thank him and inquire if it's okay to ask him a final question before I go. He looks at me and says yes.

"The Crime Prevention Law of 1954 states that governors in Jordan can hold a woman in administrative custody without just procedures if her release will lead to a criminal act taking place. How does this work in practice?"

"Quite simply," he answers, explaining that the governor has the authority to decide whether the threat to the woman is reduced so that she can be released. As a rule, it's necessary for the woman to have a male guardian to guarantee her safety. This happens when the man in question comes to the prison and signs a document in which he promises that the family will not harm the woman and that they will pay a fine of five thousand Jordanian dollars—approximately seven thousand US dollars—if they break this promise.

I sit in silence, doing the calculations in my head. To put this sum in context, the average Jordanian earns about 33,000 US dollars a year. In other words, the fine corresponds to a little less than three months' wages.

"Seven thousand dollars for a life," I exclaim.

He leans forward and says that the exact amount doesn't matter if the family has decided to kill her anyway.

"But who acts as a guardian for these women, then?" I ask, thinking that the only people who can get these women out of prison are most likely the same ones who want to kill her. The purpose of the law—to prevent crime—therefore no longer applies.

"Fathers. Brothers. Perhaps a husband," he responds, confirming what I had already thought—that the law isn't designed to protect the women—but to get them out of the way.

"But aren't they the exact people who want to take these women's lives?"

He confirms that that's true but that it is the duty of the man to ensure the woman's safety, and that no authority in this country should deprive a father or husband of that responsibility.

The comment is disheartening. I look at the self-assured man who is working in one of the most important ministries in the country when it comes to women's safety. He obviously believes that a woman is the property of a man and that her family has the right to decide what to do with her.

"Women lose no matter what," Amina had said when we met in the desert. Now, I understand more and more what she meant. Not only am I myself sitting stuck in the middle of the Jordanian bureaucracy, but I have also seen how deeply rooted the discrimination is—even at such a high level in the system.

***

THE DOCTOR HAD known what was going on before they even managed to say anything. Why else did two girls come to the hospital alone in the middle of the night? They must be afraid of their family, said the slightly older man in a white coat. He had a mild voice and friendly eyes, and took Aisha and Amina into his office.

Right away he asked Aisha if she was afraid of someone hurting her, and she told him that she was terrified that her mother and father were going to kill her. The information spilled out. She asked the doctor for help, told him about the panic attacks, about how she tried to tell her lungs to breathe but that her body ignored her and her throat collapsed so it felt like she couldn't get enough air and was going to die. The doctor calmly told her that it sounded like a perfectly common panic attack and that you can't actually die of such a thing. It was good they'd come, he said, but this wasn't a problem a doctor could help them with, so he called the police. There was a situation they had to "clean up," Amina heard him say.

Aisha told the doctor that they weren't interested in reporting the case. They didn't want to involve the police; she just wanted help with her physical ailments.

But the doctor ignored her, and before they were able to do anything at all, two police officers came into the office and said they were going to take Aisha with them.

Amina protested loudly. Aisha needed medicine—some pills that could calm her down—not a conversation with the police. They didn't want to report their father or make the situation any worse than it already was. She couldn't understand how the police could help in this situation.

"We can't protect your sister here at the hospital," the doctor said. "It's a job for the police. She'll get protection in prison."

Aisha's eyes widened. She pressed her mouth shut so hard her lips quivered. She started breathing faster.

"No!" she cried out in a kind of strangled scream, jumped up from the chair, and tried to run toward the door. The closest policeman positioned himself in front of the door, grabbed her, and held her. She started to hyperventilate.

"We don't need your help," Amina said. "Just forget that we came."

The doctor shook his head. The authorities would take care of Aisha, he said. She would be safe now.

Amina jumped out of her chair and hurled herself at the policeman who was holding Aisha. She tried to tear her from his grip. She used all the muscles in her body and acted on pure instinct.

"Let go of my sister!" she shrieked, clawing at the policeman's arms.

The other policeman grabbed her around the waist, pulled her away from Aisha, and put her face down on the ground. She felt his knee hit her spinal cord, and a hot pain ran from her leg up to her neck. Her face was pushed down into the floor, and she turned her head to one side to avoid breaking her nose. Terrified, she stopped resisting and lay still, convinced that he was really going to hurt her. She lay there, unable to move. From the corner of her eye, she could see the other policeman carrying Aisha out of the room, as she kicked her feet and gasped for air. Then the door shut. Amina's eyes filled with tears. The floor beneath her became wet and she felt her cheek grow damp, but she didn't make a sound. She just lay there, helpless, feeling the weight of the policeman on her shoulders. She said to herself that she had done the only right thing, that the authorities would take care of Aisha just as the doctor had promised, that she wasn't at fault for whatever was to happen to her sister.

When she thought back on the situation, she knew that Aisha had been put in indefinite custody that night and that their trip to the hospital was perhaps the biggest mistake they had made in their lives.

The fact that Aisha ended up in jail only made the situation worse. The rumors started to churn. Soon everyone knew that Aisha had been involved in immoral behavior and that Baba was willing to kill her. She had had a relationship outside of marriage, someone said. She was pregnant, said others. The neighbors talked. The family was in shock.

Baba and their mother never forgave Aisha and Amina for what had happened or how they had handled it. The family was now put in an impossible situation in which they had to act. Aisha was in just as much danger in prison as she was at home, since Baba could demand to have her released whenever he wished, as long as he promised he wouldn't hurt her. People expected Baba to restore the family's honor. Aisha had ruined him.

Amina particularly remembered coming home after the night at the hospital. It was seven o'clock in the morning when she finally walked through the door and saw Baba sitting slumped over the kitchen table with his head in his hands. He'd been informed about what had happened before she made it home. It was clear he had been crying. He didn't say anything to her, but his eyes said it all. His daughters had betrayed him. He was accused of being willing to kill his own children, forsaken by the one person he had opened up to. He shook his head and turned his gaze away. After that, he'd never been able to look at her properly again. Amina felt like her heart would explode from guilt.

THEN, THE DAYS had turned into weeks; the weeks, into months. Now here she sat, thinking about everything that had happened in the last six months and waiting for Aisha to come home. Baba had been at the police station and signed a document so Aisha could be released from prison. He had promised he wouldn't hurt her and said that he forgave her for what she had done. It would be nice, her mother had said as she tidied their room and baked a cake that they would eat when Aisha got home. The whole house smelled like bittersweet cinnamon and ginger. The scent made Amina nauseous.

She was terrified of what she feared was about to happen. She had tried to sleep away the reality for the last week, and dreamt a great deal. Different faces had turned up in her mind and disappeared in a kind of strange fog. Fragments from her childhood buzzed around her head like short films on a TV screen. She saw Aisha running along the beach at the Dead Sea and catching insects, the sun rising in the east over the oak tree above Amman, Baba lifting Aisha up and giving her a pale yellow sunflower for her fourteenth birthday. She wrote some of the memories in a notebook so she wouldn't forget them—or perhaps she wrote them specifically to forget. She wanted to disappear from the present and preferred to think of the memories that were still worth remembering.

She was unable to look forward to Aisha coming home and felt an indescribable apprehension in her body—a feeling like it was already too late. As though her childhood was about to be ripped away from her.

There was something that didn't add up. Baba hadn't forgiven her after all. He hadn't made eye contact with her in six months. He hadn't spoken to her or acknowledged that she was in the house or even a part of the family. So why would he have forgiven Aisha? He blamed her for everything—for his honor being insulted and for people now thinking that he was a bad father.

Amina knew that Baba would never forgive them for what they had done, and that he would never forgive himself for having shared the secrets of his past with her. Why would he want his daughters—who had so egregiously betrayed him—home again? Why would he want them around him at all?

Amina rocked back and forth on her knees in terror. She already knew the answer to that question.

***

I'M DRIPPING WITH sweat on a chair outside the office of Eva Abu Halaweh, the executive director of the Mizan Law Group for Human Rights, after a chaotic morning in the rush hour of Amman. I'm late to our meeting. The office was difficult to find, even though I'd been there several times before. My GPS stopped working when I needed it the most, and a grouchy cab driver had driven me into all of the city's dead ends, detours, and traffic jams as time ran away from me. I looked up pictures of Halaweh while I sat in the taxi, growing even *more* stressed when the first picture that came up was one of her with Michelle Obama and Hillary Clinton.

I look around the little waiting room. A row of chairs is standing along a wall that is covered with posters bearing the organization's logo and the various services they offer. "Legal Aid Program" one of them reads, followed by the text: "Mizan provides long-term solutions for women in danger, especially those who are placed in administrative custody (Jwaideh Prison). We offer necessary services such as housing, legal assistance, and conversations, and we encourage women to demand justice and protection from violence in close relationships, including those at risk of being killed in the name of honor."

I read over the text several times and am once again filled with admiration for this little organization, which was started in 1998 by local lawyers and jurists who wanted to raise awareness about human rights in Jordan and provide legal assistance to vulnerable communities. It is because of their tireless work that I understand the legal framework for honor killings at all. Together with journalist Rana Husseini, the organization is almost single-handedly responsible for all the information it is possible to obtain in English about the subject. They worked toward amending (and now hope to abolish) article 340, and for a number of years have documented how the regulations discriminate against women and are in violation of human rights. They have started campaigns and organized demonstrations in opposition of the article. They have engaged the international community, which has led to the article being up for hearing in court several times. Their work truly makes a difference.

On the chair next to me is a young woman dressed in an olive-green dress, looking blankly around the room with a registration form in her hands. I wonder what she's doing there. For my own part, I'm here to verify Amina's story.

The woman at reception comes to me and explains that Halaweh unfortunately had to go to another meeting. She says that Fatima Al-Halabaya, whom I have met several times before and who works as a psychologist and therapist for the organization, can meet with me instead.

The receptionist guides me through an office with light-blue walls, past three cubicles with tall stacks of paper and court documents, and over to Halabaya's area. I look up at the shelves, which are jam-packed with pink folders and black binders. On the desk is a heap of papers just like the one the woman next to me in the waiting room was holding. Black-and-white photographs are stapled to the tops of the documents. A woman with a roughed-up face is at the top of the pile.

I look at the endless sea of paper around me and realize that I am surrounded by women with stories just like the one Amina told me. Here they are, all filed side by side, pile by pile. The room is filled with fates from floor to ceiling.

"So nice to see you again," says a familiar voice behind me. I turn and meet Halabaya's friendly gaze. She greets me with outstretched arms and gives me a kiss on each cheek. Being both a psychologist and a former police-woman, she is strong and easygoing at the same time. She gives me a long hug. I comment that it looks like she has a lot to do. Her shelves have gotten significantly fuller since I was last here just a few months ago, I point out. Halabaya confirms that I am unfortunately correct. She looks tired. The entire shelf to the right of her desk—about seven to ten feet high—is filled with rape cases.

"All these girls," she sighs. "There are so many young girls here."

I look at the tower of paper. The number is overwhelming.

"What brings you here today?" she asks, and wonders whether I've gotten any further with my work. Have I visited the Jwaideh Women's Prison as I'd planned the last time I was here?

I explain that I'm still waiting for permission from the authorities but that I have a concrete story, which I'm wondering if she's perhaps worked with before.

I tell her about Amina, explaining that her sister was killed but that she survived, and that I've spoken with her father, who is still alive. I show her photos of the article that was written in the paper after the killing, which I've found in the immense archives at one of the local newspapers.

"It's one of the worst cases I've ever worked on," I admit, feeling that the emotions associated with all of this reality are difficult to hold back. Halabaya is the only person I know who truly understands the scope of the problem; she works with the same issues every day.

"Don't you get sad working on all these stories?" Halabaya asks, clearly having registered my feelings. "Don't you lose faith in the human race?" She takes off her glasses and rubs her eyes.

I look alternately at her and at the piles of paper that surround us and pose the same question to her as my vision grows blurry—because she's absolutely right. When I sit here and see the extent of the issue, in this office with files from floor to ceiling, being able to do something about it feels completely hopeless.

"Yes," I reply. "But then—there are also people like you."

I think of the enormous difference Halabaya is making for all of the women in these folders. She saves lives every single day, despite threats and judgment from the community. Halabaya's life has been threatened several times by furious men and women who say they're going to kill her because they believe the women she's trying to save deserve to die.

"You do what you can," she replies, and confirms that she knows which case I'm referencing. She asks how I've even managed to speak with him, Amina's father.

I answer that it feels like the only proper thing to do, and that he has the right to have his voice heard, but that I'm having a difficult time presenting what he's done in an objective way.

"Why doesn't he regret it?" I ask.

Halabaya points out that it's impossible to objectively relate to the actions of a killer, and that regret is very complicated. "You can't expect to find remorse in someone who doesn't feel guilty about what they've done." Then, she points out that remorse is a complex phenomenon that also depends on culture. Moreover, it is linked to a number of psychological processes. If a person regrets something that can't be undone—for example, taking someone's life—it's natural for that person to justify or explain away the act, for instance by viewing themselves as a victim in order to reduce the pain.

"Have you confronted him about the killing?" she asks, and I admit that I haven't asked him about it directly yet.

Halabaya reminds me that I shouldn't have too high an expectation for how he'll react. He'll likely just try to explain away what he's done.

"But there are also some who feel remorse and want to atone for what they've done," she says, placing her hands on top of the heap of paper. Since 2007, she has been working with just these kinds of cases. Cases in which children and parents want to forgive, understand, and reconcile. She's worked with women who need help getting out of prison. With brothers and fathers who have threatened their sisters and children but later regret it and want to reestablish contact with them.

Halabaya says they spend a lot of time getting children and parents to speak to one another again. First, they help the women get out of jail and offer them security, psychological follow-ups and a secret address, but as time passes, they try to put children and parents in contact with one another again.

"When sorrow and anger have subsided, most people are able to forgive each other and reunite," she says.

That's probably the only permanent solution if you are going to have a chance at survival, I think. Jordan is a small country where rumors spread quickly and everyone knows their neighbors. Moreover, a single woman without a connection to any father figure, brothers, or other family will ultimately be looked down upon. The chances of living a normal life with a job and a new family would be minimal.

Halabaya leans toward me and says the story I'm referring to is unfortunately not one of the cases in which reunification has been possible. Amina was willing to forgive and wanted to meet her father after so many years apart, but Mizan thought that the situation was too risky and advised her to stay in hiding. Halabaya says that she remembers the case well and asks me to be careful—for Amina's safety as well as my own.

"Can you put me in touch with her again?" I ask.

Halabaya hesitates, shakes her head, and says it's difficult, at least in cases like this one in which the woman's life is still in danger.

"Don't forget it's a killer you're talking to," she advises. "And don't forget that this is Jordan."

CHAPTER 4

A GOD FOR THE BLIND

"MET MY DAUGHTER?" Rahman says. "You're talking to the wrong person. I don't have any daughters. They died a long time ago."

I stare at him. For two years, we've been meeting each other in the same cafe in Amman and speaking about the same story. For two years, I've looked him in the eyes and listened to his thoughts about honor killing, faith, and tradition. I've lied to him, and he's lying to me—now that I'm finally telling him the truth.

"I've spoken with your daughter," I repeat. "Her name is Amina. Her sister was named Aisha. Your name is Rahman Abd Al-Nasir. You killed your mother when you were eleven years old, and shot your daughters when they were sixteen and eighteen."

He gets up and starts swaying from side to side with his eyes shut. He holds onto the table tightly with both hands like he's about to lose his balance.

"Are you all right?" I ask, getting up and putting a hand on his shoulder.

"Don't touch me!" he hisses, pushing me away. He slams his hand on the table so hard that everyone in the cafe turns to look at us. "You don't know what you're talking about. You've got the wrong person. Who do you think you are?"

He raises his voice and waves his index finger in my face. It swings from side to side so aggressively that it looks like a fan before my eyes. I ask him to sit down again, to give me the chance to explain. If he disappears from the cafe now, I'll lose the story again—just as quickly as I lost Amina.

"I know the scar on the right side of your face is from when you killed your mother. Sit down, Rahman Abd Al-Nasir. I know you're the right person."

He looks around nervously and leans across the table. "Be quiet!" he snarls. "I have no daughters. You're speaking to the wrong person."

I look at him and understand what's about to happen: he's going to leave. He's going to disappear into the busy streets outside the cafe, hurry up the narrow alleys, through a gate, a door... and I'll never be able to find him again. The story will end here. In this cafe, with this familiar scent of Arabic coffee and apple tobacco. The search for information has turned; he and I have switched sides now. He's going to find out where I live, who I've been in contact with, and the names of everyone who has worked with me.

I try to apologize, to explain the confrontation. I say that there are many people with the same name here in Jordan, and that it's easy to make a mistake, that maybe he's right.

I try to make him feel safe again, but none of what I say seems to have any effect. He straightens up, tosses a few coins on the table, and shows signs of being on his way out. I beg him to take my Norwegian phone number. "In case you change your mind," I say. "You can always call." I take out a scrap of paper and I write down my number, but he refuses to take it.

"Jordan is small," he says, full of disdain, and turns his back to me. "I'll find what I want. Who I want," he mumbles, and walks away.

I sit at the table as he disappears out the door. I want to follow him and find out where he lives, but I know I've already crossed a dangerous line. I see the top of his head bobbing up and down among the other people out there. Up through the alleys, into the dark streets, all the way to a place he calls home. Perhaps it's even the same home where Amina and Aisha grew up.

I sit in the cafe, wondering whether we're ever going to meet again, and whether I can still use what he's told me even though he's now denying parts of the story.

I pull out my list with the 139 names of women in Jordan who were killed in the name of honor between 1995 and 2014. Aisha is represented in one of the 139 rows on the sheet. "Killed for immoral behavior," it reads on the blurry pages I found in the archives of *The Jordan Times*. The official story was of course different from what Amina told me. In the papers it said that Aisha was killed for adultery—a reason for killing so obvious, so excusable, that most Jordanians wouldn't even react to it. In contrast, no one has ever been officially killed for homosexuality in Jordan. Such a shame would never be mentioned to the general public. Such numbers can't even be found in the statistics. Immoral behavior such as adultery, pregnancy outside of marriage, rape, or just a bad reputation, however, are all causes for killing that are well represented on my list.

I sit, musing over what Rahman thinks about what he did. I wonder whether a father who killed his own child is even still in touch with his feelings, and whether he feels remorse.

Maybe he doesn't. Maybe he's never needed to accept responsibility for the lives he's taken. And what is a crime without punishment? What is a criminal who never gets judged?

I REALIZE THAT I have revealed and confronted Rahman with everything I know and that this will have to be my last evening in Amman. I'm not safe here anymore. A killer who walks free is undoubtedly dangerous to have any association with. I pack up my things, leave the little cafe, and start down the long road back to the hotel. I walk quickly through the hectic streets in downtown Amman, squeezing among the spice and fruit stalls with their good deals and loud voices. The women smile at me when our eyes meet. After many years in the street scene, I've been allowed to take part in a kind of silent community of women. I don't know them and they don't know me, but we see each other, smile, and wink like we're old friends. It wasn't like that the first times I lived here, I think, and feel a bit melan-choly now that I have to go home and may never return.

I haven't seen Amina in three years, and will probably never see her again—if she's even still alive. I have tried to recreate what little she told me and confirm the various leads I've gotten, but just a couple of hours of recording have given me little to go off. The police won't give me any answers. The Public Security Directorate wants me out of the country. The various organizations I have worked with can't give me any more information than I already have. And now Rahman has disappeared.

The story ends here, I think.

***

THAT SAME NIGHT, I'm lying awake in the dark with my eyes wide open. I can't sleep. Thoughts are whirring around my head. I've spent three years looking for guilty people in a country where no one seems to want to admit guilt or take responsibility for what they've done. I've spoken with men who were forced to kill their mothers when they were only children, boys who were pressured to take their sisters' lives, and husbands who tortured their own wives to death. What they all have in common is the feeling that they—just like the women they killed—were themselves victims of honor killing, and therefore blameless.

I think about Rahman. He also denies all accountability for what he's done. He denied it all and ran away. It hadn't been the confrontation I'd been hoping for. It felt like he'd escaped—once again.

Why has it been so important for me to hold him responsible? I wonder. Do I have some subconscious need to punish him on Amina's behalf? Or is it remorse I'm looking for? The remains of *some* kind of humanity. Something you could grab onto to effect change.

The calls to prayer resound over the towers of the closest mosque and mingle with the cold night air. I turn on my side and stare out into the pitch-black room. My gaze lands on a strange shadow at the door. I squint to make my vision clearer. In the crack between the door and the floor, I can see an undeniable shadow. It looks like someone is standing there, right outside my door, with both feet pointing in toward the room. I stare at the shadow, trying to figure out if someone is actually standing there, as I frantically try to find the phone without turning on the light.

Someone knocks on the door, and suddenly I feel like I'm back in the hotel room in Aqaba in 2013.

"Open up," says a familiar voice, then adds my name.

It's Rahman. He must have followed me back here from the cafe.

He knocks on the door again as I sit in the dark, terrified. He's going to kill me, I think, feeling for the hotel phone on the nightstand with shaking hands. I lift the handset and repeatedly press the operator button at the top. The beeping fills the room. I feel like he can hear me. He knows I'm in here. He knows that I can't come out.

"Someone's trying to break into my room," I whisper when someone at the reception desk answers.

"Should I call the police?" the receptionist asks. I immediately reply yes, but then change my mind the next second. It's going to take too long to summon the police—and they have no right to arrest him. "Is there someone who can help me now?"

"I'm sending up security," says the receptionist.

I put the phone down, get up, and tiptoe silently to my purse, which is sitting next to the door. I search for my pepper spray, find it quickly, and stand there with my finger on the trigger in the dark, prepared for him to break in.

We stand that way for a while, he and I. Just a foot and a half apart. Separated only by a door.

"I have more to say," he says. "I'm going down to reception. You can come if you want to talk to me."

I see the shadow outside move and hear the sound of steps disappearing down the hallway. I stand there, confused. I've almost stopped breathing entirely. It's impossible to know what he wants. If he had wanted to harm me, he would've done so here, not sat down in the reception area where other people could see us, right? The adrenaline is pumping through my veins and my hands are shaking. I fall down on my knees and try to think clearly. Maybe he really *did* just want to talk. I think about the situation. The confession I've been looking for all these years might be moments away, but how much am I willing to risk? My thoughts are interrupted by someone hammering loudly at my door and pulling at the doorknob.

"Everything okay in there?" says the security guard, who must have sprinted from reception.

I stand up again and put on the jacket that's hanging over a chair by the door. "It's okay, I think," I say, opening the door to see a man who looks like an Arab boxing champion standing on the other side. He looks around the room to make sure I'm alone, then asks what happened. I explain that an acquaintance tried to break in, but that he eventually left without doing anything. He looks at me in surprise.

"Do you have a weapon?" I ask.

The man holds out his hands, shakes his head, and says he doesn't need one. He has these, after all, and flexes his muscles.

I think for a moment. Maybe I can go down to reception and see what Rahman wants if this giant of a man comes along and protects me? I ask him if he saw an older man on his way up, but he just shakes his head and says he hasn't seen anyone at all. I explain that the man who was outside my room is waiting in the reception area, and that I want to speak with him, but he may want to harm me.

"Can you protect me if something goes wrong?" I ask.

The man answers yes. Of course he can. It's his job, after all.

"Great," I say, sticking my feet into a pair of sneakers and finding my notepad. The enormous man turns and I scurry after him down the corridor, simultaneously terrified and high on adrenaline. Part of me wants to just barricade myself in my room for the rest of the night, book tickets home, and get out of the country as fast as possible—never to return. Another part, however, simply has to meet Rahman one last time.

"Can you check if he has a gun?" I ask the man, and he looks at me skeptically.

"Do you think he's armed?" he asks. "Then I have to check. We can't have people with weapons inside the hotel."

We walk down the stairs and enter the reception area.

I stop when I see Rahman's familiar posture. He leans forward, with a slight bend in his back, as though he can't fully manage to bear his own weight. He is wearing the same clothes as when we met in the cafe earlier that day. The dark green jacket hangs like a tent over his narrow shoulders.

"That's him," I say to the guard, pointing, and meet Rahman's eyes. They are red, and it looks like he's been crying.

The guard strides toward him and says something to him in Arabic. Rahman lifts his arms over his head and holds my gaze as the guard searches him. He looks weary. Tormented.

The guard stops the search and speaks calmly to Rahman. Then he turns to me, nods, and signals that he isn't armed and that I can talk to him now. I cross the room, still maintaining steady eye contact with Rahman.

"How did you know where I'm staying?" I ask when we're facing each other.

The guard stands a few yards behind us, following the situation closely.

"I followed you," Rahman answers, and apologizes. He was set off by the question in the cafe, he explains. He didn't know that I'd spoken with Amina. He didn't even know that she was out of prison, or that she was still alive.

"You were lying to me!" he says, shaking his head. "The whole time."

We sit down at one of the tables in the nearly empty room. I apologize, and try to explain that the only thing I lied about was the fact that I had met Amina. I tell him I hadn't dared to tell him the truth right away because I was afraid he would do precisely what he did—run away.

He looks down and fiddles with my pen, which I've set on the table. "How is she?" he asks and exhales heavily.

I'm a bit taken aback by the question. "I don't know," I reply honestly. "It's been three years since I saw her."

He sits in silence, staring into space. Then he rests his head in his hands and says he doesn't want me to write a book about him after all. He doesn't want to be portrayed as a murderer. That wasn't why he shared all this information with me.

I tell him that we've made an agreement and that his identity will remain anonymous. I emphasize that he voluntarily met up with me all these times and chose to speak about all the topics we've been discussing.

"You can't take back what you've told me," I say.

He seems irritated by this, and leans forward and asks me what right I have to steal his story. The story of his life.

"It's not just your story. It's also Amina's."

He narrows his eyes. "You have no respect," he says coldly.

I ask him if he can give me the pen he's fiddling with. I want to write down the last things he has to say about the matter. I flip to a blank page in the notepad, stretch out my hand, and add that he has one last chance to explain himself.

He drops the pen onto the table and puts his hand on top of mine. We sit like that for a moment, in a kind of strange gesture I don't fully understand. I look at his fist, rough and calloused, and the scar on his face. We sit there for a long time, without either of us saying anything at all.

"I have no explanation," he says at last.

I pull my hand back, discouraged. The first thing I think is that three years of research and interviews can't end like this. He *has* to have an explanation. There *must* be a reason. Then I realize that maybe he's right, because maybe there *isn't* any logical justification. No excuse, no remorse. Perhaps his conscience has been taken over by vindictiveness, just as it was the first time he was beaten by Baba and learned that everything that was painful and difficult, complicated and intangible, could be replaced with honor. Perhaps Halabaya was right in that I couldn't expect to find remorse in someone who doesn't feel any guilt for what they've done. Perhaps he has his own logic and rationale that he relates to. Because there *was* a reason that he did this, after all.

"How did you restore your family's honor?"

"I killed my daughter," he says, and tells me the little he can remember from the day that changed everything.

As he speaks, I notice that something about him has shifted. His gaze is turned downwards the whole time, and he sits in thoughtful silence for long periods, as though we are avoiding talking about what he really wants to say and he's waiting for some kind of decisive judgment to be passed upon him.

I listen, but never ask Rahman if he regrets what he did. For remorse requires recognition and the ability to be open to forgiveness. Not just from yourself but also from Allah. But Rahman has never acknowledged or forgiven himself for what he believes he was forced to do—and Allah is a hope for forgiveness I'm sure he does not believe in.

"I am a victim," he repeats several times as he tells me what he did to his own children that morning.

It never ceases to amaze me how little honor and pride was left in his eyes when he said that.

***

"WHAT KIND OF a man are you?" Noora had said repeatedly for the last month. "Your son is going to grow up in disgrace. Your daughters are mocking you. You have to do *something.*"

In the end, Rahman simply couldn't stand any more nagging. It was either his wife or his daughters, he thought as he lay in bed one night, exhausted but unable to sleep. He'd had enough. He had been commanded his entire life, controlled by expectations, pressured by his family, his clan, or society. What kind of honor was there even left to defend? He had been a broken man from the start.

Yet he wondered how his children could betray him this way. What had he done to deserve such daughters?

Aisha had lied to him, been sneaking out at night, meeting someone before she was married. Amina had known it the whole time and had not said anything. She'd helped Aisha cover up the lies. Both of them were just as guilty. Both of them deserved the same punishment.

He asked himself whether there was a way out, whether there was another solution—but he couldn't see any other alternative. The community would shun the entire family if he didn't act now. They would get evil looks and comments from the neighbors. Everyone he knew would think that he had failed as a father and that he hadn't managed to protect the most precious thing he had: his daughters and his honor. They would view him as a man without the ability to defend himself. And only by punishing those who had taken his honor could he prove that he was able to defend his interests again.

He was broken by the whole situation. He'd been terrified of having daughters from the day he found out he was going to be a father, always afraid that something would go wrong. Because if something goes wrong with a woman, it's always the men who have to pay the price, the men who have to act. He had feared that a day like this would come, that he would be pushed into a situation where the only thing to do was to kill his own children.

Had it not been for society's expectations, he wouldn't have needed to do this, he thought. Then he might have been able to just lock them up in the house until someone married them or they eventually died alone. That wasn't really a fair choice, though; killing them was the only thing he could do. It was better to sacrifice two daughters than the whole family. It was just as his father used to say: a drop of dirty blood is enough to destroy a whole bottle of good milk.

It had been easy to get hold of a weapon. He'd spoken with Nasir and asked him what he would do, and he'd gotten the handgun the next day. Didn't he want a bigger weapon? Nasir wondered, but no, he was sure that a .45 caliber was enough.

Nasir said that he would've shot both Aisha and whomever she was with, but Rahman disagreed. It wasn't his job to clean up other families' messes. Whomever she was meeting wasn't his problem. He only cared about his own daughters. His own son. Akram, who was completely innocent in all of this, shouldn't have to go through exactly the same thing he had as a child. It couldn't happen again. It was enough now. He couldn't fail Akram as he'd been failed by his own father.

"I'll do it," he'd said to Noora when he woke up that morning. Her eyes filled with tears. For a few moments, he was unsure of whether it was from grief or relief. Perhaps it was both. They held each other and cried together before he got dressed and went down to the kitchen. He made coffee and went out into the garden, where he spent the end of the early morning beneath his fig tree.

Then he decided to chop it down. It would only remind him of his mother and daughters, he thought. All these women. All the betrayal. He fetched his ax and hacked with all his might at the thick trunk until it broke in two, and the tree fell to the ground with a crack.

Afterwards, he stood in the kitchen and stared out of the window at the piles of branches that now lay heaped around the courtyard. The calls to prayer flooded from the towers. The traffic, car horns, and people's voices in the streets formed a deafening mass of sound that blended with the whirring of the fan spinning from the ceiling. He looked at his reflection in the window, exhausted. There had been too little sleep over the last few nights. He had been lying awake wondering what to do. But now he had decided.

For a brief moment, he wondered what his mother would think of him now if she knew what he was about to do. Just the thought of her made him furious.

He doesn't remember any more than that, he'd told the police when they had come after it was all over. From the time the first reports of screams coming from a house in Amman were reported on the police network to the time the police officers stood outside the house, over an hour had passed. The shots had showered through his children. He doesn't know how many bullets he fired in total, but one hit Aisha in the head before it burst the artery in her throat. That was what had killed her, the autopsy report concluded.

The bullets had also pierced through Amina's pink nightdress. Blood dripped from the holes, and parts of her face were gone. But she was still alive. Her eyes were wide open. And she was staring at him. As though it were his fault that he had to kill them.

The police took Rahman with them while Aisha and Amina were taken away in an ambulance.

For one of them, life was already over.

For him, all three of them were already dead.

***

ONE EARLY WINTER morning, Amina saw Baba fetch the ax and chop down the huge fig tree in the garden. He chopped at the thick trunk with his powerful upper body. His face was somber and his eyes were red. The sharp blade hit the juicy meat of the trunk so chips flew in all directions. With each swing, a cloud of leaves fell to the muddy ground. He chopped deeper and harder until the tree wobbled on a narrow twig in the middle. Then he cast the ax away, pushed his fingers through his hair, and dried his forehead. The old tree wobbled in the air, leaned to one side, and fell with a bang.

Amina looked at Baba's strong arms, at his angry face and his red eyes. She grew anxious again. The atmosphere in the house was tense. It felt like they were waiting for an inevitable punishment that could strike at any time. She sat down on her bed and stroked her fingers over the smooth silk sheets. On the wall hung the drawing that Aisha had made for Amina when she turned seven. It showed the two of them together under the big oak tree with the view over Amman. Two stick figures holding each other's hands.

Why had she snitched to her mother that morning in Aqaba, when she knew deep down what the consequences could be? She had been so hurt, so afraid that her own life would be destroyed. She had taken on the shame as if it were her own. It wasn't because she wanted to help Aisha that she'd tattled to their mother; no, she wanted to get rid of the problem, not to have to deal with it, to put responsibility on someone else and make sure she kept her *own* honor intact. But now, she thought there wasn't any honor in the choice she'd made. She had chosen to save herself for the price of her own sister. The worst thing was that she knew Aisha would never have done the same.

She smelled the scent of Baba's strong morning coffee spread across the house. She heard the sounds of Aisha washing up in the bathroom. She peered out the window again down at the garden where the enormous tree lay with sap dripping from its open wounds. Then she heard another man's voice. Perhaps Uncle Nasir? Or was it Akram she heard down there? She heard the sound of quick steps on the stairs that first scurried up, then down. Then her door flew open, and Uncle Nasir stormed into her room. She met his stern gaze and felt the powerful hands that grabbed her and dragged her out of the room.

She could hear Aisha screaming, but she herself was numb. Paralyzed. She had no questions and needed no answers. She knew what was about to happen. It felt like she was sleeping. Like this was just a bad dream, and that she would wake up tomorrow in her own bed after a nightmare. She wished she had the courage to scream, but she couldn't.

She looked Aisha in the eyes as she was dragged into the living room. She could see how she fought with her arms and legs as Baba and his brother tied her to a chair that stood back to back with another chair. They were the dining chairs Baba had bought in Syria. The ones Aisha had painted white.

She looked down at the pink lace nightdress she was wearing. She'd gotten it as a birthday gift the day she turned fourteen. She looked at the kitchen knife. The handgun. And Baba. Her dear Baba, who was now stuffing the towel they used to dry the dishes with into Aisha's mouth. She gurgled. Retched. Thrust her head from side to side and spat the towel out. She howled that Baba had said he would always forgive her, that it was Allah she should fear. Not him.

"You're my *father*!" she screamed.

Amina was pushed down into the other chair. Her hands were pulled backwards and tied to Aisha's. She tried to twist away but was stuck. Her body had no power, and the shock had rendered her virtually immobile. She started to panic. She screamed with all her might, but only a wheeze of air came out. She wanted to shout so the neighbors would hear it, so someone could save them, but she had no voice. She opened her mouth again and again, pushing as hard as she could to make a sound, but her breath just went inward. She was hyperventilating, and it felt like she was drowning.

Suddenly, she felt a thump on her head. Everything disappeared, and for a long time everything was dark and quiet. Then, a glittering appeared before her eyes. She woke up again, sat there confused, swaying from side to side. She couldn't quite understand what had happened. She opened her eyes and saw Baba through a stripe of her own blood. She could see the drops hit her thigh.

Baba picked up the knife and came over to her. He slashed the knife into her somewhere between her breast and stomach. She felt it break through skin and tissue when he pushed it in and pulled it back out. Her whole body twitched. Her throat, lungs, and mouth filled with blood, but she could still breathe. She could still feel. It was an indescribable pain.

Baba turned his back. Now he'll stop, she thought. Now they've gotten their punishment. For a moment, she sat up and thought, look, now you see, she was right, he wouldn't dare, he just wanted to scare us. She tried to straighten up to show she wasn't afraid. She knew he wouldn't go any further now. Only a blind man is innocent of the things he cannot see. And Baba knew that it was wrong to kill them.

Then, she felt her sister let go of her hands, and she heard the crushing sound of her sister's body falling to one side.

She stared up at Baba, who stared back at her.

He was holding the pistol. Aiming it at her.

Then he closed his eyes.

HOW THIS BOOK
CAME TO BE

THIS BOOK TOOK me four years to write and it raises a topic that will take me a lifetime to understand. To me, honor killing is an act that is just as contradictory as the term itself. As though "honor" can ever justify "killing."

I have based the book primarily on what the people who were present during these events told me happened. I've used a variety of data collection methods such as participatory and non-participatory observation, qualitative interviews, quantitative surveys, document analysis, and audio recording. I have strived to get all the information confirmed by secondary sources, such as newspaper archives, court documents, autopsy reports, others' accounts, and various other sources on the topic. However, several scenes have only one narrator, and some of the information has simply not been verifiable. Some details and descriptions of a person's thoughts and emotions are also my own interpretation, based on my own experiences and reasoning from similar situations and places.

Through my work on the book, I have built close relationships with some of the sources. Such a fusion of journalist-informant relations and personal experiences provides good data but at the same time can make it problematic to interpret information objectively. I have therefore chosen to write myself into the text because I think it is better to be honest about the kinds of positions I took with me into each situation as a journalist than to present a selection of facts as neutral information.

I met Amina once—in Wadi Rum in Jordan in November 2012—and she was the one who wanted her story to be published. She agreed to meet with me to talk about her sister, Aisha; the time she had spent in prison; and the injustice she feels she was exposed to. It was important for her to assert that the Jordanian legal system indirectly encourages individuals to take the law into their own hands, and that when we met there was in practice no alternative for women who want protection against honor killing in Jordan. "Honor killing has nothing to do with sharia, the Quran, or Islam," she said. For me, the most important question was what could cause a father to kill his own children if it didn't have anything to do with religion.

Amina's story is based on the conversation we had and on the two-hour Arabic tape recording she gave me. I naturally didn't have the opportunity to pose any follow-up questions to the information on the tape. Accordingly, I have based her descriptions on what she has told me, what her acquaintances have described, and what I have seen and observed in Aqaba, Amman, and other places in Jordan.

I have interviewed activists, lawyers, and the police, and searched for written sources to verify that what Amina has said is true. When I confirmed from various sources that the murder of her sister happened as she described it, I decided to move forward with the story.

I immersed myself in the legal framework and the events that led to Amina ending up in prison. I went to the neighborhood she grew up in. I walked through the streets she frequented. I visited many of the places she described and spoke with several of the people she would have known. I went to local prisons and police stations, and I tried repeatedly to get inside the Jwaideh Women's Prison—without success, even after I marched into the Public Security Directorate's offices to personally request a response to all of my applications.

After writing Amina's story, I tried to understand her father's motives by reading the Quran, hadith, sharia, the Jordanian penal code, books about the Jordanian legal system and the history of Jordan. I acquainted myself with the ancient traditions and culture connected to honor, traveled through the desert to Petra and Wadi Rum, and learned how the clan structure in Bedouin society works. I gathered statistics and facts related to honor killing and documented all of the honor killings I came across in legal documents and newspaper archives. I ended up with a list of 139 names. I tried to get in touch with the siblings, fathers, and mothers who had taken the lives of these women—to ask them *why*.

I spent more than a year trying to find Rahman. I asked if he was interested in meeting me to discuss matters related to honor. He was skeptical but eventually came to an interview when I said that I wanted to talk to him specifically because he was a well-respected man in the neighborhood. We met for the first time in January 2014, and I proceeded to interview him seven times over a period of two years. From the very first meeting, he was informed that I was writing a book and that I wanted to publish what he told me as long as he was willing to contribute. I guaranteed that he would get his part of the manuscript delivered to him for review before the book was sent to press. He said yes. He was very interested in explaining the concept of honor and its function in society, and to discuss so-called Western delusions about Islam. He agreed to share stories of his own upbringing and personal experiences as long as I could guarantee his anonymity.

I tried to either confirm or disprove the information Rahman gave me by speaking with local imams, sheikhs, acquaintances, or older village leaders. I have had trouble verifying parts of his story beyond his own depictions. For example, in public legal documents or archives, I find no trace of Masuma's killing. Because of the credibility I have established in everything else Rahman told me, however, I have decided to trust that what he says is true—including this part of the story.

I held back the information that I had spoken with Rahman's daughter until our second-to-last meeting, which resulted in him initially not wanting to contribute to the book anymore. The reason was first and foremost the story about his mother, and the fact that Amina could express herself in the book and clearly describes what he did. Rahman does not want to be described as a killer, nor does he want to seem weak or shameful. His desire to withdraw the information has of course been an ethical dilemma for me, both as a journalist and a fellow human being. However, the story I have written doesn't just belong to him, but also to his daughter. He had already given his consent for the information he shared to be published. I have therefore—since the people are anonymized and I consider the story to be important—chosen to move forward with the book. Rahman has received repeated offers to read the manuscript and give me corrections, but he has not answered any form of inquiry since our last meeting in Amman. I traveled back to Jordan one last time in November 2016 to deliver a translated draft of the manuscript in person, but he doesn't want to talk to me anymore.

Protecting my sources has, of course, been extraordinarily important. Amina's life is still in danger. She is still at risk of being killed if her uncle and brother realize that their story has become public. Rahman still risks imprisonment—and in the most extreme consequence, the death penalty—if the authorities find out that he killed his mother and was never punished for that crime. In addition, third parties such as Maram, Uncle Nasir, and Akram are also at risk of grave consequences.

The names, family compositions, geographic references, times, ages, genders, and other information that may help identify Amina, Aisha, Rahman, and other family members have therefore been changed or omitted.

The resistance I have met from the authorities in connection with the work of the book has been immense. It took me three years to get answers to my applications. I have been met with criticism and closed doors, and I have been monitored and encouraged not to return to the country. In certain situations, I have had to circumvent the law, such as when I entered the prison in Aqaba.

OVER 36 HONOR killings were reported by the Jordanian government in 2017. This may seem like a small number compared to an overall population of 7.9 million people, but the numbers are rising and the rate of change represents an 89% increase from the 19 deaths reported in 2002. Moreover, there is most certainly a huge number of unrecorded cases. It is my hope that heightened awareness of these issues and international pressure to change the laws that discriminate against women in Jordan can help reduce these numbers in the coming years.

In the name of justice and human rights for women and girls in Jordan, I call on the government and political and legal authorities in Jordan to:

- Prohibit reduced penalties in cases related to honor killings, regardless of whether or not the victim's family calls for leniency.

- Set up a national system to track and report on how many honor killings are committed. The data should include the reasons for the killing, the relationship between the attacker and the victim, whether or not a formal complaint was filed, and the sentences handed down against the killer and any accomplices.

- Adopt a comprehensive national strategy to prevent violence in the name of honor, to protect those at risk, and to prosecute anyone involved in this kind of violence.

- Work with activists, local women's rights organizations, religious and community leaders, police officials, social workers, teachers, and health workers to protect potential victims, and to help combat discriminatory attitudes.

- Protect—not punish—those at risk of honor violence. It is vital that women who are put in safe shelters are free to leave whenever they decide to do so. At the moment, these women cannot leave the facility without permission from the administrative governor, and being effectively locked up in a safe shelter instead of a prison does not make much of a difference. Being locked up anywhere against one's wishes is a violation of human rights. The authorities should imprison the perpetrators and potential perpetrators of these crimes, NOT the victims!

- Abolish the Crime Prevention Law of 1954 which gives governors the right to put women in protective custody. No governor or "male guardian" should have the right to decide when an "honor situation" is safe enough to release a woman from protective custody. In some cases, family members have pledged not to harm women in protective custody—only to kill them after they've been released.

- Tackle the deep-rooted discrimination that reinforces the concept that female "moral" behavior is paramount for upholding the honor of their families and communities—and the expectation that male family members will prevent and purge any transgressions of honor through violence.

THANK YOUS

A S A JOURNALIST and author, I am incredibly humbled by the generosity of everyone who has helped
me understand this topic. Without the help of
friends and acquaintances in Jordan, this book would have
been impossible. Through their local knowledge and contacts, I was able to get access to the most important archive
in Jordan—the rumor mill. They put me in touch with all
the right people, patted me on the back when I wanted
to give up, and reassured me when I was threatened or
suspected of something. They have put their own lives
and reputations at risk by digging around in these matters
and asking after these people, and thrown themselves into
my work with an enthusiasm that has driven the project
forward.

A special thanks to Ms. Fatima Al-Halabaya for her
untiring work at Mizan. Amina and Rahman, for their

courage and honesty. Lubna Dawani at Sisterhood Is Global Institute (SIGI), Sissel Birgitte Breie, Moe Suleiman, Alhani Mohannad, Tareq Amear, Samir, Nusair, Attalah Huwaitat, and Rana Husseini, for their knowledge, support, and assistance in Jordan.

Thank you to everyone at Kagge Forlag. My editor, Marius Fossøy Mohaugen, for professional input and guidance. Erling Kagge and Anne Gaathaug, for the invaluable enthusiasm they have shown for my manuscript.

Thank you to Rania Maktabi, Nora Mehsen, Mats Bleikelia, and Åshild Eidem for their edits and feedback on the manuscript.

Thank you to Fritt Ord, which supported my last fieldwork in Jordan and made it financially possible for me to complete the project.

Thank you to Robert Fisk, Gavin MacFadyen, and Angela Phillips, who taught me to ask questions and opened my eyes to investigative journalism.

I would also like to thank everyone who has lived with me and this book for the last four years. Family, friends, and colleagues. Mom and Dad, who taught me to seek justice. Marlene, who helped me believe that a project like this was possible at all. Unn, who has been my home when I no longer had one myself. Ida, who made me want to finish the book and come back to my life. And Grandma, who unfortunately passed before the book was finished but who still protects and inspires me. Thank you! All of this depended on you.

REFERENCES

Preface to the English Edition

Article 340, Penal Code of Jordan, no. 16, 1960

1. A husband who surprises his wife or one of his female descendents or ancestors or sisters in the act of adultery or in an illegitimate bed and immediately murders her or her lover or both of them, or assaults her or both of them and the assault results in death or injury or harm or permanent disfiguration, shall benefit from a mitigating excuse.

2. A wife who surprises her husband in the act of adultery or in an illegitimate bed in their home and immediately murders him or his lover or both of them, or assaults him or both of them and the assault results in death or injury or harm or permanent disfiguration, shall benefit from the same mitigating excuse mentioned in the paragraph above.

3. The right to self-defense shall not be used against whoever benefits from this excuse and the provisions of aggravating factors or circumstances shall not apply against such a person.

Article 97, Penal Code of Jordan, no. 16, 1960

When the law provides for a mitigating excuse:

1. If the felony is punishable by the death penalty or by life imprisonment with hard labor or life detention, the penalty shall be replaced with imprisonment for a minimum of one year.

2. If the act constitutes any other felony, then the penalty shall be imprisonment from six months to two years.

3. If the act constitutes a misdemeanor, then the penalty shall not exceed imprisonment for six months or a fine of twenty-five Dinars.

Article 98, Penal Code of Jordan, no. 16, 1960

Whoever commits a crime while in a state of rage which is the result of an unjustifiable and dangerous act committed by the victim, benefits from a mitigating excuse.

Article 99, Penal Code of Jordan, no. 16, 1960

If mitigating factors existed in a case, the court shall rule as follows:

1. Life imprisonment with hard labor or ten to twenty years of temporary imprisonment instead of the death penalty.

2. Temporary imprisonment for no less than eight years instead of life imprisonment with hard labor, temporary detention for a period no less than eight years and instead of life detention.

3. The court has the power to reduce any other criminal sentence by half.

4. Except in case of repetition, the court may also reduce any penalty that has a minimum limit of three years imprisonment to a sentence of at least one year imprisonment.

Human Rights Watch reports that, as of 2016, "Penal code articles 98 and 340, which allow reduced sentences for perpetrators of 'honor crimes,' remained in force." (Human Rights Watch 12 Jan. 2017).

See Canada: Immigration and Refugee Board of Canada, *Jordan and the United Arab Emirates: Treatment of divorced women, including those living with their ex-husband, by family members and society; information* on honour-based violence, including state protection (2015-August 2017), 15 September 2017, ZZZ105955.E, available at: http://www.refworld.org/docid/5afadec54.html [accessed 26 September 2018].

See also Rothna Begum, "How to End 'Honor' Killings in Jordan," Human Rights Watch, April 3, 2017, https://www.hrw.org/news/2017/04/03/how-end-honor-killings-jordan.

"The Jordanian Parliament voted on Sunday to remove the mitigated excuse offered under Article 340 of the Jordanian Penal Code to 'honor-killing' murderers." This means that the mitigating excuse offered under Articles 98 and 97 can no longer be used in rulings regarding honor killings. The vote was applauded by civil society and human right activists attending the session.

See Jassar Al Tahat, "MPs approve amendments to controversial Article 98," The Jordan Times, July 30, 2017, http://www.jordantimes.com/news/local/mps-approve-amendments-controversial-article-98 and "Parliament makes amendments to 'honor-killing' article," Roya News, July 30, 2017, http://en.royanews.tv/news/10977/2017-07-30.

In a 2017 document submitted to CEDAW's sixth periodic report of Jordan, Jordan states that "[s]entences handed down in honour-motivated homicide cases, where mitigating circumstances were taken into account, have not been less than imprisonment of 10 years according to data derived from court judgments" (Jordan 11 Jan. 2017, 14).

Country Reports 2016 notes that, at Jordan's Supreme Criminal Court, "cases involving honor crimes in recent years routinely imposed prison sentences of up to 15 years to perpetrators of such crimes," but that the "Cassation Court, which reviews the Supreme Criminal Court rulings, generally decreased the sentences by half" (US 3 Mar. 2017a, 32). The same source also states that the "Supreme Criminal Court issued one ruling on an honor crimes case during the year, sentencing a father to one year in prison for killing his daughter" (US 3 Mar. 2017a, 32).

See Canada: Immigration and Refugee Board of Canada, Jordan and the United Arab Emirates: Treatment of divorced women, including those living with their ex-husband, by family members and society; information on honour-based violence, including state protection (2015-August 2017), 15 September 2017, ZZZ105955.E, available at: http://www.refworld.org/docid/5afadec54.html [accessed 26 September 2018].

Introduction

p. 20: ... *lead to a criminal act taking place.*

Article 60, Penal Code of Jordan, no. 16, 1960

1. Execution of one's right is considered as any act deemed necessary due to an imminent need to prevent an illegal and unprovoked offense against his/her person or property or the property or person of others.

2. The protection shall be equal for both natural and legal persons.

3. If there was an encroachment in the defense, the perpetrator of the crime might be exempted from penalty according to the conditions stipulated in article 89.

Article 89, Penal Code of Jordan, no. 16, 1960

Whoever commits an act out of necessity to protect him/herself or others or his/her property or the property of others from a significant and imminent danger shall be exempted from punishment provided that he/she did not willingly cause such danger and his/her action is congruent with such danger.

If the victim's family drops a complaint, even that one-year minimum can be cut in half. Some perpetrators in Jordan have been jailed for as little as six months for killing a daughter or sister. (AP 24 June 2017).

According to the Director General of the Jordanian Women's Union, as cited in a 2016 article in *The Jordan Times,* another clause of the penal code "allows families to drop charges against perpetrators, which leads to reducing the sentence by half" (*The Jordan Times* 1 Dec. 2016). In April 2017, the same source reported that courts "often reduce sentences because the victims' families request leniency. This is usually the case as members of the victim's family are often complicit in 'honour killings'" (*The Jordan Times* 1 Apr. 2017). Similarly, *Country Reports 2016* indicates that when the victim's family chose not to pursue the case, the government completely dismissed proceedings. In 'honor crime' cases, the family of the victim and the family of the alleged perpetrator were often the same, since the perpetrator and victim usually were related (US 3 Mar. 2017a, 32–33).

See Canada: Immigration and Refugee Board of Canada, *Jordan and the United Arab Emirates: Treatment of divorced women, including those living with their ex-husband, by family members and society; information on honour-based violence, including state protection (2015-August 2017)*, 15 September 2017, ZZZ105955.E, available at: http://www.refworld.org/docid/5afadec54.html [accessed 26 September 2018].

1. The Red Shoes

p. 12: ... *passersby would agree with him, according to statistics.*

"The Global Divide on Homosexuality," Pew Research Center, June 4, 2013, http://www.pewglobal.org/2013/06/04/the-global-divide-on-homosexuality and "Global Views on Morality," Pew Research Center, http://www.pewglobal.org/2014/04/15/global-morality/table/homosexuality.

p. 24: ... *the right to stone another person.*

The only thing the Quran says that could be considered close to an order to stone someone is that the Prophet's (PBUH) method of punishment should be used for adultery. There is also a part of hadith that says that Muslims in the time of the Prophet stoned two people for adultery. No hadith states the Prophet himself took part in these kinds of punishments. However, when there is talk of God's judgment, God rains stones down on humankind.

3. Once and for All

p. 130: ... *Jordan's population is Christian, while 97 percent are Muslim.*

Central Intelligence Agency, "Middle East: Jordan" (see Population), *The World Factbook*, https://www.cia.gov/library/publications/the-world-factbook/geos/jo.html.

p. 134: ... *written in* surah *11, which is called* Hud.

Surah 11 contains 123 verses, but the relevant ones here are 69–83. The relevant sections of *surah* 7 are 80–84.

See *Noble Quran*, https://quran.com/11/69-83 and quran.com/7/80-84.

p. 139: ... *a step in a more liberal direction.*

The penal code was amended in 1951 to decriminalize private adult and consensual acts of sodomy.

See Australia: Refugee Response Tribunal, JOR34990, June 23, 2009, http://www.refworld.org/pdfid/4f5defd92.pdf and Aaron Magid, "Little Protection for Gays in the Middle East," *Al-Monitor*, August 12, 2014, https://www.al-monitor.com/pulse/originals/2014/08/jordan-homosexuality-gay-lesbian-rights-lgbt-conservative.html.

p. 141: ... *law and order is prohibited.*

See Australia: Refugee Response Tribunal, JOR34990, June 23, 2009, http://www.refworld.org/pdfid/4f5defd92.pdf and Aaron Magid, "Little Protection for Gays in the Middle East," *Al-Monitor,* August 12, 2014, https://www.al-monitor.com/pulse/originals/2014/08/jordan-homosexuality-gay-lesbian-rights-lgbt-conservative.html.

p. 143: ... *acceptable in certain situations.*

"The Global Divide on Homosexuality," Pew Research Center, June 4, 2013, http://www.pewglobal.org/2013/06/04/the-global-divide-on-homosexuality and "Global Views on Morality," Pew Research Center, http://www.pewglobal.org/2014/04/15/global-morality/table/homosexuality.